This book paints a picture of not just how unique everyone's path in life is, but also how so many people end up on a field somewhere. It shows and encourages the young ones to dream and to chase those dreams.
—Alex Hugo, USA Women's National Baseball team captain and starting second baseman

Thank you for embracing my dad and bringing historic facts to light again.
—Mrs. Deborah James, daughter of Bobby "The Rope" Boyd

There is so much nostalgia and Americana in baseball, especially in Kansas. Capturing just some of those stories and celebrating the past and future of Midwest baseball in the process is something special.
—Katie Woods, tournament director, NBC World Series

The writing about my grandfather is truly phenomenal.
I laughed, cried and walked down memory lane.
—Kimberly Knox, granddaughter of Bobby Boyd

I know you enjoyed the brewery content in your first book, but baseball is your first love. As much as you tell individual Sunflower State stories, the book's also a bit of a love story about your passion for the game. That makes it relatable, as anyone who picks up this kind of book would surely share your love of the game.
—Chris Orlando, editor (son)-in-law

Kansas BASEBALL

MICHAEL J. TRAVIS

THE
History
PRESS

Published by The History Press
Charleston, SC
www.historypress.com

Back cover: (*Center*) League 42 sidewalk logo. Author's collection.

First published 2025

Manufactured in the United States

ISBN 9781467158749

Library of Congress Control Number: 2024950016

To Mark, my older brother, who will be present in my life always,
joining me on Rock Chalk walks, the next Strat-O-Matic game,
and as I embark on new writing journeys. You were a true storyteller, always
searching for the next wonderful story, enthusiastically immersing yourself in the
moment, in the lives of others, eager to capture the essence of people,
sprinkling the magic of your stories near and far. Whenever I bake chocolate chip
cookies or whoopie pies, I will eat one for you.

I will love you always.

To Jude Everett, Luna Grace and Jonah Rory—simple moments with your grandchildren often become your most priceless memories. I look forward to endless moments with each of you in the years ahead.

It's a kids' game, and that never changes.
—Mike Roberts, manager of the Cotuit Kettleers, Cape Cod
Baseball League

Baseball, it is said, is only a game. True.
And the Grand Canyon is only a hole in Arizona.
—George Will

People ask me what I do in the winter, when there's no baseball.
I'll tell you what I do. I stare out the window and wait for spring.
—Rogers Hornsby

Put me in, coach. I'm ready to play today.
Look at me, I can be centerfield.
—John Fogerty

Mike Travis slugged a double to aid the cause.…Shortstop Travis
was a defensive stalwart.…Mike Travis laced an RBI triple.
—Rick Harrison, *Andover Townsman* sportswriter

I've learned that the game is more than just a sport—it is dreams
and aspirations for so many youngsters everywhere I go.
—Jean Fruth, visual storyteller/cofounder of @Grassrootsbaseball/
author/Global Sports photographer

CONTENTS

ACKNOWLEDGEMENTS

This book would not have been possible without the love and support Ivy threw my way while she immersed herself in year one of her graduate school journey at Rockhurst. My love for her knows no bounds, like a fine wine slowly opening in the decanter of life.

Doors opened on my research journey, key to developing a story with a strong baseball heartbeat. My gratitude goes out to my doorkeepers, including Stacey Lattin of the Hopping Gnome, Katie Woods, Curt Nelson, Dayton Moore, Anna Kimbrell and Brent Kemnitz.

What would I have done without the endless support provided by my teammates at Rainy Day Books, the no. 1 indie bookstore in the Midwest? I look forward to the launch event in March 2025!

I have had opportunities to collaborate with wonderful artists who have magically impacted the richness of *Kansas Baseball*. Thank you, Lexi Fox, for your vision and efforts to make me look younger as we walked among the brick warehouses in the West Bottoms. Thank you, Megan Grace Day, for bringing baseball enthusiasm to your creative work displayed throughout the book.

My older brother, Mark (author extraordinaire), gave me newfound confidence, providing westerly winds to open my sails. Thank you for your encouragement!

Anna Kimbrell, a member of the USA Women's National Baseball team, brought her southern hospitality my way in a wonderful conversation. She became a baseball trailblazer while growing up in her home state of South Carolina, intent on "just playing ball." In her sixteenth year as a member of the USA team, her love for the game has not wavered. I tip my cap to Anna for all the clinics and mentoring she dedicates her time to.

Later in the book, you read about Bill James's (Sabermetrics) dislike of editors. I have been blessed to have Chris Orlando (my son-in-law) play a leading role in both of my books, serving as my editor with unwavering dedication.

I am proud to give my younger brother, Phil, recognition. Having his eyes on my manuscript as well has given me a burst of energy!

To Lennie, Jim, Steve, Rusty, Frankie, Anne, Tony, Andy, Paul, Dave, Kevin, Joey, and Charlie, thank you for creating the great sandlot baseball memories of our Little League days in Andover.

I had a fortuitous moment on my last day at Eck Stadium. I met Charlie Lord, a volunteer at the World Series, a great ballplayer back in the day for the Washburn Ichabods and Topeka Aces, a writer and a new friend. The stitches in a baseball are the red threads that can connect fans of the game in ways not anticipated. Charlie, thanks for stopping by!

It took two *New York Times* best-selling authors, David Von Drehle and Joe Posnanski, to remind me that there cannot be a book about baseball in Kansas without Bill James's story. You spoke, and I listened!

Chad Rhoad, senior acquisition editor with The History Press, has provided me the platform to have two books published. Chad, I am forever in your debt for getting behind both book proposals, bringing the talented team at Arcadia Publishing along for the ride. I offer a heartfelt thank-you to Ashley Hill, my copy editor for *Kansas Baseball*. Ashley impacted the quality of my writing and was so thoughtful about my book.

Alex Hugo, captain of the USA Women's National Baseball team, has brought her intensity and fire to my book and our ongoing chatter. Alex, I look forward to sharing a stage with you where you can show off your latest silver medal from the 2024 Women's Baseball World Cup while we talk baseball at a venue yet to be determined in your hometown of Olathe.

Indie bookstores are priceless. I clap my hands and bow to each of you for providing shelf space for *Kansas Baseball*! Shout outs to The Raven Bookstore, Flint Hills Books, Red Fern Booksellers, Watermark Books & Café and Monstera's Books for making a difference in the reading lives of your communities.

The next time I see a great blue heron flying overhead, it will give me the opportunity to look toward the heavens and thank my mom, Marty Travis, for the life she gave me and for the mother-son bond that will never be broken. Mom, I hope that you are proud of me.

I saved the best for last. I am blessed to have three wonderful women in my life. To my wife, Ivy, and two daughters, Katie and Meg—I love each of you forever.

Let's play ball!

INTRODUCTION

Welcome to the Travis Wiffle Ball Park, located at 62 Elm Street in Andover, a northern suburb of Boston. The white, three-story home of the Travis family towers over the "ball field," offering shade on scorching summer afternoons. What memories I have of those magical times.

The field, demarcated by a tar driveway showing its age through winter frost fractures, had a number of unique features, reminiscent of the hometown heroes park, Fenway on Lansdowne Street. The mound was centered in the driveway, parallel to the two stone steps that guided the thirsty competitors up to the sidewalk leading to the back porch and a pitcher of Kool-Aid. The plate, roughly twenty feet from the mound, was a street hockey goal that offered a liberal strike zone, the backdrop the tiny two-car garage with a seasoned plywood backboard looking down at the action, jealous that wiffle ball was the game of choice during the summer months.

The batter, stepping in with the yellow wiffle ball bat, looked down the left field line, teased by the short porch at the foul line. His eyes wandered deeper toward the outfield fence, green hedges stretching from left to right, only interrupted by the driveway spilling onto Elm Street. To clear those four-foot-high hedge walls would take quite a drive, pushing the white ball high and deep.

The game was played with the rhythm of a summer song. The smack of the bat, the pitcher shifting to cover the entire field, running back with visions of scaling the hedge to steal a home run from his friend, echoed against the stone wall running down the right field line.

Playful chatter lifted in the air as the pitcher, a Nolan Ryan wannabe, called his pitch before winding up, while the batter dug in, calling out that "Yaz" was stepping to the plate, batting cleanup. Playing wiffle ball with a best friend is pure enjoyment, time slowly cruising by, while celebrations of long home runs, cries of disbelief at defensive gems witnessed by screeching blue jays and the overarching and restless limbs of the right field foul pole (an aging oak tree) hang in the humid August air.

I loved those days, greeting my best friend Charlie at the back screen door, charging down the steps to the "dugout," a spot under the back porch where the wiffle ball gear was haphazardly stashed after the last at-bat the night before. We would play wiffle ball every moment we could leading up to the late afternoon, eagerly awaiting the time when we would head our own way to pull our little league uniforms on, soon to meet back at the Playstead fields, now opponents in a more serious game.

That love for all things baseball manifested itself through the next five wonderful years that I lived at 62 Elm Street. My first glove was my first love, with a pocket full of dreams of being a big leaguer caught in its web. I was hopeful that I would land with a Brooks Robinson infield glove; instead, due to demand and/or cost, I came home with a Bobby Knoop special that I learned to care for and love as my little league years progressed.

I was a lucky kid, having the opportunity to stir up a medley of baseball journeys, starting with our wiffle ball matchups. When I found myself alone, the backyard would call my name. I would venture out back, squeezed in by a swing set and our neighbors' property, as I tossed tennis balls high in the air, chasing down each lazy fly as it bounced off the roof of our home. I was a shy kid, so the idea of stepping on the mound in a little league game horrified me. Those fears didn't stop me from pitching on my own, with two options, to either wind up and throw at a small cellar window underneath our dining room bay windows or haul the pitching backstop onto the driveway, knowing that accurate throws would come back at me in the form of sharp line drives. I was an early version of Greg Maddux, never witnessed.

I vividly remember my dad driving me to Phillips Academy in Andover, parking outside the cages, an inside athletic space that was dark, bordered by mesh netting for our little league tryouts. I was a young nine-year-old trying out for the Major League level. Despite my shyness, my abilities to hit line drives, throw accurately and chase down grounders with ease made a loud presence. That evening, the phone rang on the wall in our back hallway. I could hear my dad answering it, his deep voice carrying to our TV room. Next thing I knew, I was called to the phone, nervously saying hello to a man that, in moments, became my first childhood manager. Coach Driscoll welcomed me to the team. It was rare for a nine-year-old to make the Majors; it was one of the best days in my young life.

It took three years for the Pirates to find their way, to shed two losing seasons, rattling off eleven wins in a row to win the National League pennant in 1973. The core of the team had matured, becoming seasoned eleven-year-olds who played key positions for Coach Driscoll's Pirates. During the summer, I would devour our local paper, a weekly treasure trove of Andover news, hoping that I would see "Mike Travis" in print, with my game action glorified by the beat writer for the paper. My chest burst when I read action verbs attached to my name, such as spiked, slugged and laced!

Another memory, vivid, painful and full of regret, comes to me every year as spring brings the game I still love back to the stage. In 1973, our Pirates not only won the pennant but also went on to win the town championship.

We lost game one of a best-of-three championship series. I found my own way to the field for the second game, learning from Coach that I was playing shortstop and batting leadoff. I stepped to the plate, in the moment, with tunnel vision focused on the opposing pitcher. On the first pitch, a swing,

The Pirates, 1973 Andover, Massachusetts Little League Town Champions. The author is seated on the far left of the second row. *Courtesy of the Andover Townsman.*

great contact, I left the box knowing that I had hit a liner heading over second base. I doubled, my heart hammering in my chest, eleven-year-old excitement bursting from my eyes. It was then when I looked out past the bleachers to see our family pulling into the parking lot in our blue Volkswagen bus. My excitement dampened as if a blanket of rain had been dropped on just me, standing on second base, alone with the memory. I share this with you because it is part of my psyche, my heart and my baseball memories. It also embodies the stories that will unfold for you as the chapters slide by. Baseball is a game that consists of love and heartbreak; the game is beautiful because of the range of emotions it can stir up, encounter, embrace.

Baseball becomes part of us. The game is magical. This book gives me the opportunity to share my love for the game through twelve amazing chapters, all connected to our wonderful state of Kansas.

I trust that your emotions are coming alive as I reminisce about the beautiful game of baseball that I love. You are about to begin a journey across our Sunflower State, reading wonderful baseball stories that all have roots in Kansas—some you will know, but others will startle and surprise you. Enjoy each story, share those surprising revelations you have with other friends and family members who love this game. When you turn the page, a wonderful map of our state will present itself. On this map, the state outlined, embracing fields of wheat and a field of dreams, has baseballs calling out the locations presented in each of the chapters in this book.

Before we turn to the first chapter, I want to share a story about the League 42 Foundation, based in Wichita.[1] Bob Lutz, the founder of League 42, and his dedicated team have been on a mission for over a decade to bring urban boys and girls into the game of baseball by minimizing the financial burden the game can place on a family, which is a dream crusher to many. League 42 pays homage to Hall of Famer Jackie Robinson, who broke the color barrier in 1947 with the Brooklyn Dodgers. Jackie, no. 42, continued to push for social change, fighting discrimination and working with others to break down barriers to life and its opportunities after retiring. His wife, Rachel, and daughter, Sharon, have continued to strive to make the world a better place through their efforts and life work. Sharon wrote a book, *Jackie's Nine*, that powerfully pays tribute to her father and the nine values that were important to him—and potentially life-changing for all of us. The nine values are displayed on permanent banners surrounding the Jackie Robinson Pavilion, located at McAdams Park, for all to read and reflect on. These values are *courage, determination, teamwork, persistence, integrity, citizenship, justice, commitment* and *excellence*.[2]

League 42 makes the game a possibility for the urban kids in Wichita neighborhoods. They are outfitted with great uniforms and supplied with gloves, bats and other gear they might need. I drove down to McAdams Park in Wichita to take in several evenings of league play this summer. I was struck by the pure joy so evident on the ballfields and in the bleachers.

League 42 has brought the community together to celebrate life, family and sportsmanship. These young boys and girls, who develop their understanding of the game through a year of tee-ball, mature as ballplayers as they progress through the age divisions. Each night, these stars of tomorrow shine, lit up like the ever-present lightning bugs painting McAdams Park with their own meteor showers.

To me, League 42 and all it represents and honors is where the story must begin. In honor of Jackie, his nine values are central to the book. I have had the honor of deciding which value is embodied in the stories that unfold chapter by chapter. I have digested the words and images on the banners in the pavilion. I have read *Jackie's Nine* and been reminded, once again, that the legacy Jackie and his family have graced us with is about so much more than baseball. I have cherished the opportunity to honor the game's players, coaches, innovators and leaders in this book by highlighting their stories with one of the nine values.

Remember that baseball is a kid's game. It will always be.

Enjoy!

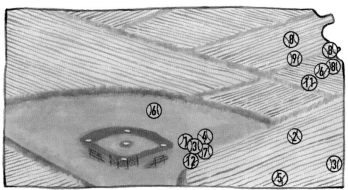

1 - Wichita
2 - Humboldt
3 - Pittsburg, Wichita
4 - Wichita
5 - Independence
6 - Olathe, Hutchinson

7 - Wichita
8 - Kansas City, KS, Prairie Village, Oskaloosa
9 - Lawrence
11- Gardner
12 - Wichita

Baseball in Kansas chapter map. *Courtesy of Megan Day Creations,
megandaycreations@gmail.com, Kansas City, MO.*

1

I MAKE HOME RUNS!

PERSISTENCE
Working toward a goal and continuing to move forward,
even though you face obstacles or barriers.

Meet the ballplayers who grace the four diamonds at historic McAdams Park in Wichita playing in League 42. Simply put, these youngsters will remind us why baseball is such a wonderful game. One of the many things these kids have in common is that they all wear ball caps that have the number "42" centered proudly on the bill. Every time they put on their uniforms, they are paying respect to Jackie Robinson and his greatness, courage and class.

- Matteo, a Panther Bear in the five- and six-year-old Lancer Tee-Ball Division: "I make home runs."

- Victoria, an A's player in the Lancer Tee-Ball Division: "I play baseball with my dad at home."

- Liam, a ballplayer for the Little Dodgers in the seven- and eight-year-old Bruin Division: "I am going to play baseball for my whole life."

- Jacob, who plays for the Magic in the Dodger Division: "We have a bunch of good players; they are really good at the game." When asked why he likes League 42, he went on to say, "It is not that much money to sign up."

- Isai, playing catcher for the Aces in the Dodger Division, had a lot to say: "I still struggle with pop flies. I am working on it. I want to keep playing as long as I can." When asked how he does in school, with no hesitation, both of his hands shifted to thumbs-up position, and he said, "I get straight As. I am good."

While I watched all these wonderful interviews be conducted by founder and executive director of League 42, Bob Lutz, a symphony of sounds tantalized my baseball-loving ears. They ranged from the happy noises of cheering from the bleachers to the clink of a bat making good contact with a pitched ball. Bob, who retired after forty-three years of dedication to the *Wichita Eagle*, including twenty-one years as a sports columnist, warmly engaged his young interviewees, exhibiting his passion and love for these kids and League 42.

Opposite: League 42 logo. *Courtesy of League 42, Wichita, KS.*

Above: League 42 action, Batter Up! *Courtesy of League 42, Wichita, KS.*

Roman, a ballplayer for the Mud Dogs in the Dodger Division, shared his feelings about why he loves League 42: "It is pretty competitive; you get to cheer on your teammates. I like all the barking because we are dogs!"

Zea, playing for the Wolves in the Lancer Division, exclaimed, "Baseball is fun, running and hitting!"

Da'Juan, outfitted in a Hawks uniform, playing in the Dodger Division, responded to a question about what he thinks the best thing about playing in League 42 is, confidently sharing, "Being a leader of our team."

Peyton, a young girl sporting the Aces uniform, playing in the seven- and eight-year-old Aces Division, shared, "I get to hit and play with my teammates."

Campbell, playing for the Cannons in the Lancer Tee-Ball Division, enthusiastically shared why he liked his field: "I like playing on a turf field because when I slide it doesn't hurt."

These interviews, available for your viewing pleasure on the League 42 Facebook page, capture thoughts and emotions these youngsters wanted to express as they moved nonstop in Bob's rocking camp chair, some pensive, some silly, some glancing at mom or dad for support and prompting.[3] It was important to share this window into their world, all brought together as a League 42 community, playing the game of baseball at historic McAdams Park from April to mid-July.

League 42, an idea that started taking shape in Bob's mind in his latter days with the *Wichita Eagle*, became reality in 2013. This nonprofit organization, fueled by Lutz's dedication and commitment to a long-held belief that all kids should have the opportunity to play baseball, had its naysayers when he explained his idea. In our conversation, Bob shared, "I saw that the opportunity was not happening, shutting out a lot of kids. You can't just price the sport out. A baseball bat, a glove, costs forever. We made it affordable; we provide most of the equipment [fee to play is thirty dollars].” Humbly, Bob went on to say “It was a simple idea. I had enough of a known name, which helped when I reached out to people. At the first meeting, only four showed up. From there, it grew to the point where we had forty-five supporters in attendance. It just kind of happened; it is serendipitous in many ways.”

> *My life is all about League 42 now. And these kids are my passion.*
> —*Bob Lutz*

As I described in the introduction, Jackie Robinson believed deeply in the nine values he lived by. These nine values are beautifully expressed in the pavilion through murals depicting no. 42 through his life, each value defined in Jackie’s words. I say this because Bob Lutz embodies the powerful word *persistence*. Bob had an idea that took flight in his mind and soul in his later years at the *Wichita Eagle*. League 42 has blossomed over the last eleven years, thanks to Bob’s *persistence* to continue moving the foundation forward, fueling the engine with more energy and finding strength from within and from collaborators to overcome obstacles and barriers.

I am a believer in everything that League 42 represents. After parking my car, I am reminded each time I come down to be immersed in all senses by a game night, that sportsmanship is the overarching mantra for Bob and the volunteers, paid field supervisors, coaches, umpires, concession stand chefs, moms, dads and six hundred boys and girls who suit up in their uniforms to play ball.

Bob and his team of field supervisors make it a point, when needed, to remind adults and the occasional child that, at McAdams Park, League 42 is focused on being respectful and supportive of every ballplayer, while cheering and celebrating the game action and eliminating any umpiring or coaching from the stands. Bob has lived League 42 every day since its inception, fully aware of the effort, dedication and positivity that have been expended over the last eleven years to create the magic that is witnessed nightly under the watchful eye of I-135, towering over two of the fields.

Lutz shared his perspective about what has been accomplished, “I know it is great, but sometimes, it isn’t so great. I am more grateful that we follow our sportsmanship rules than anything else. Sometimes we stray, we are humans. We make the sportsmanship rules well known.”

McAdams, a neighborhood northeast of downtown Wichita, is the historical center of the city’s Black community. The community, which thrived in the early to mid-twentieth century, was split in two by the construction of the highway that borders one side of the park, leading to a loss of local businesses and the erosion of vibrant residential neighborhoods. By the early 2000s, community activists started infusing a strengthening heartbeat into the area's neighborhoods, leading to a revitalization plan that took hold in 2003.

McAdams Park is the centerpiece of the neighborhoods, with League 42 providing a gathering place for the surrounding community, where evenings are rhapsodic, and the air is charged with contagious energy. These fields were once the playgrounds of youngsters like Barry Sanders and Lynette Woodward, who were running like the wind or finding nothing but net as they started dreaming big. Game nights at the park now draw retired professional athletes for a visit, a chance to remember their early glory days, with the likes of Reggie Jackson and Xavier McDaniel taking it all in. The fields are alive with kids playing the game of baseball; as dusk settles in, the occasional firefly swirls around the cap of the centerfielder, who might be daydreaming about being a star as well.

League 42 has evolved year after year, with funding support from the community and The Rudd Foundation showing up through the addition of the first turf field, a concession building with restrooms, new lights, the *Leslie* Rudd Learning Center and new uniforms in 2024.[4]

The platform that this organization is built on can be life changing. Everyone involved on the four ball diamonds will learn valuable lessons about teamwork, a positive attitude, effort, determination and having fun and the importance of community. Learning does not end once the scoreboard lights go out nor as the coaches lead their teams in a game-ending cheer that echoes across the empty fields. Across the street from the ballparks stands the Leslie Rudd Learning Center.

The League 42 Foundation has provided an opportunity for Wichita's urban youngsters to play baseball. The learning center across the street has introduced opportunities for families and their ballplayers to shift from having fun on the diamonds to having fun in a learning environment, where on-site teachers, Rudd scholars at Wichita State University and volunteers help the kids with their reading and math proficiencies and STEAM learning and encourage them to understand the power of having a passion for life and learning.[5] Under the roof of this building, education initiatives include Bright Lights (an afterschool learning enrichment program), STEAM, The Passion Project (speakers from all walks of life talk about the importance of passion), Bats and Badges and the Full Count Initiative. It is safe to say that League 42 never sleeps.

The Rudd Foundation made all of this possible through its capital leadership gift of $1 million, which funded the construction of this center.

Three years ago, funding from the foundation, the city and fundraising efforts led by League 42 were instrumental in the creation of the Jackie Robinson Pavilion. Standing tall in the center of the pavilion, a statue of no. 42 was unveiled. No doubt, Jackie's indomitable spirit has sprinkled its magic over the ballparks, the families, the kids and the community.

Every moment one is immersed in all things League 42, the benefits carry on with life lessons learned, including the pride of being a good teammate, the understanding and joy of how hard work can pay off, the lifelong friendships first formed at the park, the bliss of having fun and the respect for those great ballplayers who have paved the way. It is striking to look across the fields and see ball caps displaying no. 42, whether the bill is flat or has been molded into an aggressive curve by the hands of the ballplayer. This year, a new wrinkle was introduced by Bob and the foundation, which is an important gesture to the game of baseball, connecting these kids to heroes of yesterday who loved this game.

All jerseys have numbers on the back that honor some of the greatest Black and Latino players who played the game. This league has so much depth to it, reminding us to honor the history of the game while providing a platform for these families and kids to have not only the opportunity to play baseball but also, more importantly, the incentive and support to learn.

Check out a few of the players honored each night as the kids take the field in advance of the first windup by the home team pitcher. They include no. 1, Ozzie Smith; no. 2, Derek Jeter; no. 8, Joe Morgan; no. 14, Ernie Banks; no. 20, Frank Robinson; no. 21, Roberto Clemente; no. 24, Willie Mays; no. 44, Henry Aaron; no. 45, Bob Gibson; and no. 52, C.C. Sabathia.

On January 26, 2024, Bob, the foundation and the League 42 community came together beneath showers of sadness. Less than three years after the joyous unveiling of the Jackie Robinson Pavilion, the base for the statue of no. 42 wept concrete tears, knowing that all that remained of the statue were the cleated feet of Robinson. No longer was Jackie blessing the pavilion with the intensity, passion and drive that emanated from his bronze eyes. Thieves had dragged the cut statue off its home, deposited it into the back of a truck and hustled off into the night. Was this a crime of hate or a crime fueled by a craving for cash for drugs?

The league had not yet begun, the grass had not started turning shades of green and the uniforms hadn't been disbursed, yet an angry cloud had gathered over the park. Five days after the horrible theft, the burned, scarred remains of the statue were discovered in a dumpster at a park located just seven miles away from the scene of the crime.

How could the children who played ball at the park understand the emotions their parents expressed and the physical void at the park? They could no longer look up at the statue, strong and still, and be embraced by the life lessons and history of Jackie's life that surrounded the cold concrete base. What did all this mean? Would any good come out of it?

My hint for you, as you finish reading chapter 1, is to pause and read the words that are also on display at the damaged pavilion. The ballplayers made it pretty clear through their opening chapter comments that they love baseball, their teams, school, hitting, running, catching, leading and just being. None of this would have been possible without Bob Lutz and the birth of his baseball idea.

Many of you might be aware of what has unfolded in this Wichita community since late January 2024. Regardless, as you read the following chapters about people who have ties to Kansas and the shared love for the game of baseball, you will be reminded of the life lessons laid out in this chapter. Baseball is a hard and intricate game—as is life. No matter the fears, doubts, joys, camaraderie, innovations, pioneers, debates, controversies, long careers or fleeting moments of joy and achievement, the game of baseball will find its way to a sunny spot, a warm breeze stretching out the American flag up high, the aromas of char dogs floating in the air and the bliss of being with family, surrounded by a supportive community, bringing home the daily reminder that this amazing sport represents so much more than just a game. Turn the pages, enjoy the journey that connects baseball and Kansas again and again and share with me the love of the game and the lives we are blessed to have.

2

"THE THING JUST HISSED WITH DANGER"

Ty Cobb, Detroit Tigers Hall of Famer,
sharing his first impressions of Walter Johnson's speed pitch.[6]

INTEGRITY
Sticking to your values regardless of what you think you should do.

Hall of Famer George Sisler was once caught hypothesizing that the National Baseball Congress (NBC) and semiprofessional ball was so strong in the state of Kansas because of the multitudes of farmers across the Sunflower State. And he said with a chuckle, "Farmers like baseball."

Sisler was on to something that rings true through this book. Starting with the story that unfolds in this chapter about Hall of Famer Walter Johnson, the pattern will continue with George Sweatt, Mickey Mantle, Joyce Barnes and Luther Taylor, all of whom spent parts of their childhoods on family farms.

Meet Walter Johnson, born at his family farm on November 6, 1887. The simple, white clapboard house situated on the 160 acres where Johnson's dad worked the fields was nestled along the eastern bank of the lazy Neosho River. I have traveled through this part of Kansas, Humboldt specifically, pausing to stretch my legs on the banks of the Neosho. With the river wide and languorous during the rainy season, I could picture young Walter barefoot and full of energy, dreaming not of playing the game of baseball but, instead, catching the elusive catfish he knew were tucked up under an overhang, casting deep shadows on the Neosho.

Frank and Minnie Johnson had a strong work ethic and commitment to raising their children, grounded in the right behaviors that would help shape them into good adults later in life. They did not smoke or drink—who had time for that on a big farm like theirs, where they had to grind out their living and sustenance for their growing family. Walter knew the daily routine as a farm kid and was used to the rigidity of tackling farm chores first, including helping his dad with harvesting as he grew.

When his dad took the occasional trip into downtown Humboldt, Walter would look wide-eyed with wonder at the sights and sounds. He would glance out at a field, men blanketing the grass, all focused on a pitcher throwing a ball to the batter, waiting to swing.

Walter created games when idle time came his way, first gravitating to picking up rocks and throwing them at targets, whether they be a tree trunk, a beehive or certain pieces of clapboard siding on their leaning barn. It slowly started registering in Walter's mind as he tossed the rocks that, often—in fact, almost all the time—his aim was true, his target punished by another rock creasing the wood, scattering the hive, rattling the river rock.

The young lad walked to his one-room country school, carrying his lessons about behavior, respect, honesty and humbleness alongside his apple and sandwich, digesting his lunch while becoming known as a friend to everyone, a boy who would step into quarrels, not as an instigator but as a mediator.

As his years passed in the one-room schoolhouse, the games he played evolved as well. The school had no ballyard, leaving the next steps to the imagination of Walter and his friends. The first game that introduced him to baseball was the simple act of tossing a rubber ball back and forth over the roof of the school. Walter propelled the ball to his friends with ease, hitting the targets effortlessly.

Johnson's amazing control and aim developed without him giving it a thought. He would take the time to line up empty cans at a far distance and then walk back to where his pile of rocks stood and repeatedly fire rocks true and straight, knocking can after can off the fence post, creating a harmonious sound to him—yet a nauseating racket to Minnie, his mom, who more than likely wondered what that young boy was up to.

The game of baseball has evolved through time, more so by nomenclature than structure. What my brothers and I referred to as a game of pickle in the 1970s, with two gloved brothers tossing the ball back and forth from bases they protected, the third brother as the runner, wishing that he was as speedy as Lou Brock, hungry to safely get to the other base without being tagged, had a historical link to what might have unfolded in the dusty driveway at Walter's family farm.

Johnson, showing his skills with a rock or a ball, found himself playing a game of "one o' cat" or "one old cat" with the older boys. Whether they played the game in the dusty expanse next to their farmhouse or in the school yard, the boys set up a "home plate" and a second base. Their game required a bat as well. It was a game that was more evolved and more dangerous than ours. The goal was to hit the ball hard, and the batter scored runs every time they could run to the base and back to home plate without being tagged.

Life for the family took a turn for the worse as mother nature and a rainless two years brought their fifteen years of working the farm to a halt. The Johnsons sold the land and shifted to a house they rented in the "big city"—Humboldt.

When Walter's family decided that they had to move to California so Frank could make a better living working in the oil fields, Johnson, who was fourteen at the time, had yet to play organized baseball. Thirty-five years later, this Kansas farm kid became one of the original five greats inducted into the inaugural class at the Baseball Hall of Fame, which is tucked away between the woods, rolling hills and deep indigo lakes that surround the small community of Cooperstown, New York.

I do want to pause after shedding light on what I view as the beginning of the growth of this young man, full of the decency and thoughtfulness that was instilled in him by his parents and take us to the proverbial ballpark to celebrate a bevy of insane statistics that Walter accumulated.

Walter's dad, Frank, knew that his son had a gift, a magic arm. Walter would often share with his dad that when he played "catcher" in games of one o' cat, no one would try to steal on him. This right arm of Walter's, which grew to have mythic proportions, felt as if it was one with the baseball the first time Walter held one in the palm of his hand. It fit perfectly, "as though it belonged there."

Once his dad encouraged him to try pitching, all fell into place for the young man. He stood on the mound, shifted into a short "windmill" windup, swept his long right arm behind his back and then unleashed his arm with a whip-like motion, coming almost from a sidearm position with an easy Neosho River–like fluidity. The speed pitch that left his hand was simply frightening to those who tried to dig in to bat against Walter, the experience reminiscent of watching lightning strikes rain down onto Kansas farm country, dancing, striking, sheer power freezing one in place.

In his first start with the Nationals, Johnson's opening pitch, a speed ball, was called a strike. Davey Jones, the leadoff batter for the Tigers, said, "It was the fastest pitch I ever saw."[7]

Walter pitched for the next twenty-one years for the Washington Nationals, a perennial loser for most of his pitching career. Despite the losses that piled up for the club, the runs that remained hidden, Johnson put up amazing numbers. Imagine how many additional wins Walter could have accumulated if the earliest days of his career were bolstered with a strong lineup like the teams he played for under Manager Clark Griffith in the 1920s. Cy Young's record of 511 wins that still stands today, as untouchable now as it was then, might have been challenged by Johnson if the Nationals' lineup had an offensive vitality that was nonexistent for close to 75 percent of his career.

- 417 career wins
- 38 career 1–0 victories
- 66 career 1–0 losses
- Johnson tossed 3 consecutive shutout games in a 4-game series against the New York Highlanders.
- In one stretch of nine days, Walter pitched 5 complete games.
- Over one 80-inning stretch, he threw just three walks.
- From 1912 to 1913, he racked up a record of 68–19.
- In 1913, his seventh year with the Nationals, he was close to perfect, going 36–7 with an earned run average of 1.14, throwing 29 complete games, shutting out opponents eleven times with winning streaks of 7, 10 and 14 games!
- In 1914, in his first encounter with emerging slugger George "Babe" Ruth, he struck him out on three fastballs.
- Johnson had three seasons in which he started at least 35 games and did not allow a home run—inconceivable!
- Walter won his first game as a professional in 1907; he won his 400th in 1926.
- These personal statistics grew through a period in which his team, the Nationals, finished an average of 25 games out of first place.

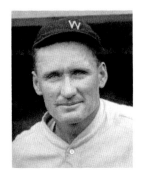

Walter Johnson, Washington Hall of Fame pitcher. *Courtesy of William Henry Jackson and Wikipedia.*

Walter racked up an astonishing 5,914 innings pitched over his career, with most of those innings and wear on his golden right arm occurring before the Nationals finally made it to the World Series in 1924. Walter, who typically would make himself available on any day he was asked to pitch, was the epitome of a workaholic. The game was not about

Walter Johnson. His selflessness was evident year after year, loss after loss. Despite losing close to 70 games by a 1–0 score, he never found fault with his teammates for their costly errors or poor hitting with men on base that could have cost him a victory. Walter had such *integrity* that he found fault in a few of his wandering pitches when he was interviewed, and he glossed over—in fact ignored—any inquiries about his teammates failing to hit or defend during the mounting losses.

Frank Graham wrote in the February 1947 issue of *Baseball Magazine,*

> *Walter Johnson had all the virtues commonly but not always truthfully attributed to athletic heroes. A simple man, he was, in his way, a great man.*

This great game of baseball, back in his playing days, embraced him as a hero, a ballplayer who came into the game with integrity and changed many fans' perspective on the tough game of baseball, historically played by ruffians. Shirley Povich, who observed Walter Johnson, captured the essence of Walter's integrity and wholesomeness in a *Sport* magazine article he wrote in 1950, titled "The Story of Walter Johnson." Povich shared that he was "captivated…by the manner of the man…while surrounded by a game that in his era was the playing field of roughnecks."

When the Nationals showed up to play away games, the fans would cheer on Walter Johnson more for the man he was than for the feared pitcher who would typically walk off the mound after a nine-inning game, once more victorious. Case in point is what unfolded in Washington, D.C., and in New York when the Nationals finally made it to the big dance, the 1924 World Series.

After Walter and his heroics helped lead the Nationals to a clinching pennant victory, he slowly walked across the field underneath a shower of cheers from across the nation, a loud rainfall of love that he tried to hide from, alone on the field, isolated, afraid to let the fans see the mounting tears filling his eyes.

At the worn-out age of thirty-six, Walter still had a stellar game, not insurmountable as he once dominated teams with his speed pitch, but good enough to go 23–7, with an ERA of 2.72 across 38 starts. He must have been tired; in fact, he was. Fans across the nation did not see Walter in his prime as he and the Nationals fought tooth and nail to win game seven and the World Series over the New York Giants. What they did see was a competitor who would do whatever was needed to help his team win.

Manager Bucky Harris shared his perspective about Walter's selflessness leading up to the World Series, stating that if Walter "could help Washington win the league, he didn't care what happened to his arm."[8]

Baseball was such a different game at the time. Before Johnson took the mound for the opening game, he described that he was "doggone fidgety about my job this afternoon, especially when you figure every last soul in the ballpark expects me to win, including the President of the United States."[9]

I was amazed at what he had to endure gracefully before the game even started! A seven-passenger Lincoln "touring car" that cost $8,000 was presented to him along with a plaque that stated, "To Walter Johnson, baseball's greatest pitcher, from his many friends."

Walter took the mound and threw 165 pitches in the opening game. He struck out a dozen Giants but was beaten down by 14 hits and 6 walks he allowed, losing the opener 4–3 to the Giants.

Game five was Walter's to win, the series square at 2–2. Pitching in the Polo Grounds was a challenge, with bleachers a short 279 feet down the left field line, 257 feet down the right field line, bookending the deepest centerfield in baseball, the wall a staggering 484 feet from home plate. Walter, in trouble for most of game five, lost again. Damon Runyon watched Walter trudge off the mound, tears in his eyes, head bowed, and wrote, "The youth was gone. By some tragic quirk of the imagination stood in his place an old fellow with stooping shoulders, as if they felt the great weight of the years, whose arms lifted wearily and fell wearily."

Astonishingly, the flip of a silver dollar determined which city would host game seven in this exhausting series. Washington won the toss. Walter was destined to take the mound once again. His beloved wife, Hazel, described the game seven experience, saying,

It was more than a ballgame to me. It was life and death.[10]

Walter threw all he could into the mix over four innings of arduous play, several times resorting to a curve ball to get out of jams, an oddity that caught the Giants by surprise. We know what eventually transpired—the Nationals and Walter Johnson won the World Series. The class and integrity that were principal in Walter's makeup were respected and celebrated, even by Frankie Frisch, who was on the losing side of the series. He called out that Walter's efforts were great and tipped his cap to the Nationals. Later in a column, Frisch expanded on those sentiments:

So long as we had to be beaten, I am glad, and so is our whole ball club,
that the victory is credited to Walter Johnson, a glorious triumph for one of
the greatest pitchers that ever lived and one of the finest, cleanest men ever
identified in baseball.[11]

I devoted a great deal of research energy into this chapter because I was drawn to this man just as the American public had been during his career. Granted, not even a Hall of Fame great like Walter Johnson is perfect, but his near perfection I admire, and I gathered a newfound perspective and insights that are impacting me to this day.

Before closing this chapter about Mr. *Integrity*, I am compelled to chronicle his marvelous opening day history with the president at that moment. The love for our country and the respect that was offered to the president of the United States back in his playing days is to be admired today, when we live in a country splintered through hate and a lack of understanding, communal spirit and empathy for all.

Walter caught seven ceremonial presidential tosses throughout his career on opening days in Washington, D.C. He typically was at his best, not only in his presidential encounters but also on the mound, winning six of those seven games. There is no doubt that without the horrors of World War I, he might have caught ten tosses.

The newspapers back in the day were glorious in their descriptions of the pomp and circumstance. Take a spin with me as we salute Walter Johnson, the "Humboldt Thunderbolt."

APRIL 14, 1910

PHILADELPHIA ATHLETICS VS. THE WASHINGTON NATIONALS

President and Mrs. Taft made a surprise arrival for the game. The presidential box was home to a large armchair, ready to embrace Taft and his three-hundred-pound frame. Walter, never one to seek the spotlight, tried to sidestep participation, happy to let his catcher, Gabby Street, take the toss. At the last moment, after Taft had risen in the grandstand, the president shifted his eyes and body and aimed his toss at Walter. The *Washington Post* shared in the next days' edition the headline: "Taft Tossed Ball—Crowd Cheers President's Fine Delivery of the Sphere." The article went on to colorfully describe the game as "such a sun-kissed, victory-blessed, roaring, rollicking, rousing opening day for the Nationals."[12]

On April 15, the *Washington Post* had this to say about President Taft:

> *He did it with his good, trusty, right arm, and the virgin sphere scudded across the diamond true as a die to the pitching box, where Walter Johnson, also the possessor of a good, trusty right arm, gathered it in, and started winding up one of his rifle shots across the plate.*[13]

Nationals win, 3–0

APRIL 10, 1913

NEW YORK HIGHLANDERS VS. THE WASHINGTON NATIONALS

President Woodrow Wilson stated, "I am deeply interested in baseball, because it is a fascinating game, because it is the American sport."[14] Wilson entered the stands amid the strains of "The Star-Spangled Banner," taking his seat in the flag-draped presidential box. Walter caught the toss; comically, when he threw it to Manager Clark Griffith, it was dropped (error on the manager!). Wilson signed the ball with a fountain pen he pulled from his suit pocket. After the game, the ball was given to Walter by a unanimous vote of his teammates.

Nationals win, 2–1

APRIL 15, 1924

PHILADELPHIA ATHLETICS VS. THE WASHINGTON NATIONALS

President Calvin Coolidge and a record crowd of close to twenty-six thousand fans packed the stands in anticipation of the home opener. Little did they know—or dream—that their beloved Nationals and star Walter Johnson would win the World Series later that year. Walter caught the ceremonial toss with his bare hand. It was a toss that caught the attention of

Walter Johnson, Washington Nationals. *Author's collection.*

Nick Altrock, writer for the *Times Herald*, who opened his story in the April 16 paper with:

> *After looking at President Coolidge throw out the first ball in the opening game here, Manager Connie Mack of the Athletics asked for waivers on him. You couldn't have hit Mr. Coolidge's delivery with the Washington Monument. I never saw such a curve. It broke before it left his hand and I thought it would break somebody's skull, too, unless it would be the umpire's, and no ball is hard enough for that.*[15]

Nationals win, 4–0

Walter Johnson brought greater crowds to baseball because of his delivery, both from the pitching rubber and the way he carried himself in public, sharing the right words with the press and public. He was the epitome of Midwestern toughness and approachability. His work ethic is demonstrated every day in the farm fields and pastures across our state by the next generation of farmers. His integrity manifested itself in the baseball greats I marveled at as I grew up, including Cal Ripken, Derek Jeter and Dwight "Dewie" Evans. I love knowing that Johnson, from the wonderful community of Humboldt, made his way to the big leagues, becoming one of the greatest pitchers *ever*.

Walter was one of the five ballplayers in the inaugural Hall of Fame class, announced in 1936. He took the stage with Ty Cobb, Babe Ruth, Rogers Hornsby and Christy Mathewson. On February 2, 1936, headlines across the country celebrated the first five.

Ironically, February 2 is an important day in my family. My younger brother Phil, Wiffle ball companion, poet, husband, dad of a bevy of dogs in Seattle and a second editor on this book journey, was born on February 2. Serendipity once again brings a smile to my face.

LOVE FOR THE GAME

COURAGE
Doing what you know is the right thing, even when it is hard to do.

The city of Wichita is where this chapter starts and ends. As I explored archives, pursued stories that were on my radar, and delighted in discovering unexpected treasures, the city of Wichita continued to manifest itself, eventually weaving its way into five chapters in this book. Why is that?

As you delve deeper into this baseball love story, you uncover a deep appreciation for the history of our national pastime in Wichita, whether it is showcased by the Monrovians, Bobby "Rope" Boyd, Hap Dumont and the National Baseball Congress, Stephenson and his Shockers or today's youth in League 42 at McAdams Park. Enjoy each story, appreciate the brave trailblazers and fall in love with a community that is coming together on summer nights to witness the magic of baseball through the sounds and sights brought to life by our youth, our next baseball generation.

Come back with me to the early 1920s. Black Wichita came out in force on game days for the Black Wonders, a barnstorming ball team who were renamed the Wichita Monrovians by Club President J.M. Booker.[16] The team was named for the capital of Liberia, Monrovia; Booker thought it was emblematic of the freedom that helped give life to a community of emancipated American slaves.

The Monrovians would take on all teams, regardless of the color of the ballplayers' skin. Games were community celebrations, drawing families in their finest, who would gather and exude an energy and pride for their team, their neighborhoods and their culture. Booker's ball club became an influential social force within the community. As they racked up wins fueled by a great mix of semiprofessional ballplayers, the opportunity arose to build their own ballpark, called Monrovian Park, that stood proudly, at the time, at Twelfth and Mosley Streets. This achievement was almost unheard of within the Black baseball world.

The mix of sage veterans and aspiring youngsters sprinted to their positions game after game, knowing that larger gate receipts would translate into better personal earnings, as well as funds needed for social causes in their community. One example of their affinity for the community was the money directed toward the Phyllis Wheatley Children's Home, established in 1920 through the efforts of Elsie Miller and the Federated Women's Club as a haven for Black children.[17] Fans knew that as they paid for tickets to watch the game, their money was also going to help the children's home and other Wichita civic projects.

The home, named after Phillis Wheatley, the first published Black poet in the country who had been brought to America as an enslaved woman in 1761, took in children from the ages of two to fourteen who could not be cared for by their parents. It was also known as a day nursery for the community, ready and waiting to welcome infants and toddlers each day so their parents could go to work.

Monrovian Park had a special feeling in those days. Families could come together, relax and socialize with no worries outside of an occasional loss for the home ball club. I imagine the love I feel when taking in League 42 action at McAdams Park mirrors what this vibrant community must have felt for their team.

Losses were few for the Monrovians in 1923. They were part of the Colored Western League, which collapsed after just one season.[18] Victories piled up as the team played in Tulsa and Topeka. It was reported that the ball club's record stood at 52–8 as August heat pushed July thunderstorms out of the way.

The team picked up where they left off, despite the collapse of the short-lived Western League, taking on all challengers. They even won a doubleheader over the all-white Campbell Merit Bread Company team, played in front of one of the largest crowds to watch a game at their home park.

In 1925, fearing trouble in the stands due to a potentially large and fractured crowd, the Monrovians purposely booked a game at Island Park on Ackerman Island. This sandbar island was located in the middle of the Arkansas River, just north of the Douglas Street Bridge in downtown Wichita.

Before we talk about the game and the controversy that swirled around it, we need to pause and pay homage to the amazing life that once was evident on Ackerman Island.[19] The island came to be in the late 1800s, the sandbar taking shape as water levels dropped in the Arkansas River. In 1890, Joseph Ackerman, owner of a slaughterhouse and packing plant, moved his family to the island, where they operated a sand business until they sold the island in 1905.

Wichita residents had a new destination for the next decade, introducing their children to Wonderland Park on Ackerman Island, a theme park that had attractions ranging from the *Great Thriller* roller coaster and multiple theaters to a roller skating rink, bowling alley, carousel and dancing pavilion. On the same grounds, Island Park Stadium proudly sat, home to baseball games.

The *Wichita Beacon* published a story on June 21, 1925, leading with the subtitle "Klan and Colored Team to Mix on the Diamond Today." The Monrovians had agreed to play a team known as Wichita Klan No. 6. Why? There was no doubt that team president, J.M. Booker, understood that there would be healthy gate receipts for this polarizing game. The state of Kansas took the lead across the country in January 1925, becoming the first state to ban the Ku Klux Klan from doing business in the state without a charter. The Klan, having failed twice to overturn this ban, were attempting to buy good will in the Wichita community.

The writers at the *Wichita Beacon* boldly declared that "strangle holds, razors, horsewhips, and other implements of argument will be barred at the baseball game at Island Park this afternoon when the baseball club of Wichita Klan Number 6 goes up against the Wichita Monrovians, Wichita's crack colored team."

The charged atmosphere at the park was subdued, thankfully, by the heavy humidity, gusting winds and unbearable 102-degree heat that settled over the park as the two teams prepared to play a 3:00 p.m. game. The *Wichita Eagle* recorded that this was the highest temperature on record for June 22. Thomas Jefferson "T.J." Young, the catcher for the Monrovians, and one of his teammates, infielder Newt Joseph, headed to their positions, uncertain of what was in store for them. The game, played evenly through the middle innings, came alive in the late innings. The Monrovians' sluggish bats, weighed down by the oppressive heat, wakened later in the game. The Monrovians held on after building a lead, winning the game 10–8. Brian

Carroll, who wrote *Beating the Klan*, shared that the game developed into "a see-saw battle" that "ended with a blizzard of scoring." No doubt, the victory engendered a sense of pride within the Black community. Ron Bolton, who writes for the website Baseball History Comes Alive, shared that the Monrovians and their fans saw the game as an "opportunity to stick it to the bigots." Bolton closed by saying, "Victory was theirs and hate had lost the day."[20]

The barnstorming nature of Black baseball at the time created many connections between ball players, as rosters shifted and evolved, with the owners intent on making sure their bus heading to the next game had enough guys to field tomorrow's team. Those circumstances led T.J. Young and Newt Joseph, who had played for the Monrovians, to make the acquaintance of George Sweatt, their new teammate with the Monarchs who was born in the same Kansas farm town as Walter Johnson.

George, born six years before Johnson, called Humboldt his childhood home. Sweatt graduated from Humboldt High well before the guns came alive in World War I but still served our country, becoming part of the Black 816th Pioneer Infantry Regiment, arriving in France with his division just two weeks in advance of the Armistice being ratified.

When he returned to Kansas, George enrolled at the State Manual Training Normal School (which became Pittsburg State University), located in Pittsburg. While working on his degree, he also found the time to display his athletic abilities, becoming the first Black athlete to letter in track, basketball and baseball. Sweatt had come a long way from the days of working in the hayfields of Humboldt, hanging up his army fatigues so he could don three different athletic uniforms, before landing as a teacher in Coffeyville.

George became a Monarch in 1922, while he was still in school, after playing well for both the Chanute Black Diamonds and Iola Go-Devils. What he earned playing ball helped fund his education, which also included classwork at Kansas State University. George played all infield positions, except for shortstop, for the Monarchs over four years. He was then traded to the Chicago Giants, where he played out the last three years of his baseball career. A highlight while he was with the Monarchs was his game seven triple in the first Negro League World Series. He injured himself stretching the gapper into a triple; the pinch runner who came in to replace him scored the winning run for the Monarchs. George went into the record books, playing in the next three World Series, one more with the Monarchs and the last two for the Chicago Giants. He became the only position player to play in the first four World Series, walking away from the diamond in three of the four seasons as a champion.

George retired in 1928 and worked for the postal service for close to thirty years in the Chicago area. Humboldt, home to George Sweatt and Hall of Famer Walter Johnson, created the Johnson-Sweatt Classic baseball tournament in 1999. Young, aspiring ballplayers now pull their gloves on and run onto the Walter Johnson and George A. Sweatt Fields, dreaming of greatness.

It is time for us to shift over to Wichita and move the clock ahead from the days George was playing for the Monarchs to the 1960s. Take a bus ride with me; let us catch a ride on the next Rapid Transit Dreamliner that

George Sweatt, Kansas City Monarchs. *Courtesy of J.E. Miller, Kansas City, MO.*

comes our way. I want the aisle seat; you can have the window so you can check out the Wichita street scene. I need to stretch my legs out and relax. I have a remarkable story to share with you. It starts with our bus driver.

Robert Richard Boyd was born on October 1, 1919, in Potts Camp, a tiny town of five hundred residents who lived near the Tippah River in northern Mississippi. Robert, known as Bobby, was introduced to the game of baseball on the weekends. Willie, his dad, and Bobby's uncle would put Bobby and his little brother Jimmy in the back of the truck on Saturdays and head down the dusty roads to play baseball games. Bobby would get creative, making his own ball out of crumpled paper and string, tossing the ball in the air repeatedly and striking line drives from his lefty stance.

Willie watched his son improve his smooth swing and hone his defensive skills at first base through his childhood in both Mississippi and Memphis. Baseball was Bobby's love, but as he grew into a young man, the last thing he thought of was playing baseball at a higher level. "We just didn't believe that was something that could happen," he said as he reflected on those years.[21] After serving two years in the quartermaster corps during World War II, Bobby found himself working in a warehouse. His love for baseball had not dimmed. He gave the game a second chance, joining the barnstorming Memphis Red Sox, a Black American League team.

Bobby was *good*, slashing at balls with his smooth swing, scattering line drives into gaps and hitting no worse than .352 in his three years with

Memphis. He led the league in hitting in 1947, played in several East-West All-Star games, earned $500 a month and worked at the Sundry Store in Memphis in the off-season.

Four years after Jackie Robinson broke the Major League Baseball color barrier, Bobby became the first Black player to sign with the Chicago White Sox. His daughter, Deborah James, shared with me that she thought of her father as a gentle giant—but not because of his physical presence. Her dad was a "trailblazer of sorts," because "he made great strides in the game of baseball at a time when it wasn't easy to do so."

Bobby debuted for the White Sox on September 8, 1951, but saw limited opportunity to play regularly. He was transferred between the White Sox and minor-league teams, struggling with the reality that his role was as a back-up and occasional pinch hitter.

Boyd remembers that the ball clubs looked for Black players "who could get along, who wouldn't be bothered if there were problems." Typically, the trouble came from the mouths of racists in the stands, who would harass these young men who were trying to make a living in the game they loved. Bobby remembered barnstorming, as one of two Black players on the White Sox. Minnie Minoso, who became the team's first Black star player, and Bobby were assigned bodyguards. Roommates on the road, the two would go to sleep in the homes of local Black families, with armed bodyguards at hand on the front porch at night to ensure the safety of the two young men.[22]

Bobby Boyd, George Sweatt and the Monrovian team epitomized one of nine values that were important to Jackie Robinson. The *courage* to take

Bobby "The Rope" Boyd, Chicago White Sox. *Courtesy of Bobby Boyd's family.*

the field in barnstorming showdowns against white teams, the *courage* to go to war in either World War I or World War II and the *courage* to turn the other cheek, to try to ignore the epithets that were hurtled at them while on the field, penetrated each of these brave men, who swallowed their pride and pushed through the injustices they were confronted with day after day, year after year.

Bobby hit his stride, with teammates referring to him as "The Rope" for his prowess in finding holes in the defense while consistently hitting above .300, whether he was playing in the Pacific Coast League or in the Winter League in Puerto Rico.

Deborah, his daughter, remembers that relatives in Memphis did not want her parents to take her to Puerto Rico, as they were fearful that she would learn Spanish before English. Her dad, called "El Ropo," led the Winter League in hitting. Their time there was a respite from the constant strife, pressures and segregation they encountered back home. She now says that was "an amazing experience" because of the respect and love they felt from the community.

Boyd's last year with the White Sox, 1953, was perplexing. He batted .297 for part of the season before he was demoted back to the Minors once again.

I spent a lot more time in the Minors than I thought I would or that I wanted to.

Would Bobby finally get a break at the big-league level, after close to four years of being shuffled around, while consistently delivering at the plate? "He most definitely, without a shadow of a doubt, had a true love of the game to endure what he endured," Deborah shared.

His big break came with the Baltimore Orioles, who drafted him from the Texas League, thanks to the recollections Paul Richards, former manager of the White Sox, had of Bobby. Richards saw big-league potential in Boyd; ironically, Bobby believed that the man who gave him the chance in Baltimore might have been one of the most prejudiced managers he encountered.

Bobby continued to persevere, showing a defensive flair, plucking the ball from the air with a snap to his glove and then shifting his attention to batting, stepping to the plate with a confidence that he could hit anything thrown his way, hitting line drive "ropes," rounding first base with style.

During the summer months, Deborah and her mom would travel, following her dad through different cities and ball parks. She looks back at the grit her dad had as he recovered from scrapes, bruises and what she referred to as "battle wounds." Not far out of reach in nearby cabinets, her dad grabbed witch hazel to help with healing, as well as the Maalox and goat's milk he took to try to soothe the chronic pain he felt during his ball playing days in Baltimore, as ulcers went undiagnosed until he had retired.

Deborah loved the traveling and adventures she experienced. Her typical ball-game dinner at the park would be pulled from a medley of options, including the classic hot dogs, peanuts, candy and crackerjacks ("I certainly didn't mind that!" said Deborah). Her mom was the manager behind the scenes, packing for the summer months, building itineraries, booking

Bobby Boyd, his baseball journey. *Courtesy of Charles Millbern*, Wichita Beacon.

accommodations and celebrating baseball on Sundays, when the family and greater community would arrive in style. "I thought it was pretty cool," Deborah said as she fondly thought of all the hats, dresses, high heels, suits, ties and polished shoes that she observed in the stands.

> *The beginning of the games was majestic to me because of all the pomp and circumstance.*

Bobby hit his stride in 1957. The year was dominated by pitchers, emphasized by the compact list of eight players who reached .300 in the American League. "The Rope" landed fourth in the batting race, delivering a .318 average for the Orioles.

Ted Williams ran away with the batting title, hitting .388, followed by Mickey at .365 and Gene Woodling finishing just three points higher than Bobby. He was not only the first Black player signed by the Chicago White Sox but also the first everyday Oriole starter in the twentieth century to deliver a .300 batting average. Amazing accomplishments for the kid from

Potts Camp, who developed his batting stroke with a stick and a ball made of shredded paper held together by a string.

Bobby was meticulous with his approach. Deborah remembers her dad taking scheduled naps on game days, rejuvenating his body, mind and soul prior to arriving at the ballpark. She remembers summer ballgames when her dad would stride toward first base in the opening inning, his cap precisely folded and his cleats polished and ready for a new day, a new game.

So, where do Bobby and the Rapid Transit Dreamliner bus merge and become one? How is Boyd connected to the state of Kansas?

Bobby retired from the Majors, worn out from the grind and the illness that sapped his strength despite the copious quantities of Maalox and goats' milk he consumed. The Rope was so disciplined at the plate that he averaged one and a half walks for every time he struck out, finishing with a .298 career average. He is still in the record books for being part of the first opening day triple play in MLB history, wearing his Orioles orange, white and black.

The Boyds headed to Wichita. Bobby saw an opportunity to continue to play baseball after unpacking in their new home. The local bus company, the Rapid Transit Dreamliners, had put together a semiprofessional company team that would compete in the National Baseball Congress World Series, held in Wichita (the next chapter is all about the NBC, its founder, the trailblazing days under Hap Dumont's leadership and the great caliber of ball that unfolded in the tournament).

Bobby played for the Dreamliners for four years and was instrumental in the success the team had, as they won the NBC World Series in 1962, 1963 and 1965. Boyd brought his charisma and style to the game, knowing that many of the ballplayers looked up to him as an elder, playing into his late thirties in a game built for younger men.

The Rope would step to the plate and toy with the pitcher, at times jumping back from a first-pitch fastball as if he was intimidated. Between shifts as a Dreamliner bus driver, his ability to drive fastballs all over the park would stun these cocky young pitchers who believed they might have the old-timer right where they wanted him. A fellow NBC ballplayer, Leonard Kelley, recalled how Boyd made deception a pure art form: "Somebody would throw him a curve, and he would about fall down swinging at it," Kelley going on to say, "Then he'd hit the next one out of the ballpark."

In 1965, Bobby was selected as the most valuable player in the tournament, hitting .409. The beauty of NBC was the matchups of former big leaguers, like Bobby, against up-and-coming youngsters who might aspire to make it in the Majors. One such match-up must be celebrated. Bobby stepped up to bat three times against the young right-hander pitching for the Fairbanks Goldpanners. Boyd went 2–3 that day off future Hall of Famer Tom Seaver.

Bobby's oldest grandchild, Kimberly R. Knox, who grew up to teach at Adams Elementary School in Wichita, basked in the warmth of her memories, sharing, "Papa was a go-getter. He was a people person who loved Tina Turner, Michael Jackson, and the Dallas Cowboys. He was passionate about baseball and instilled the love of the game in us. The card shows were exciting. Papa was always dressed to the 'nines' when he attended. I would carry his signing pens and markers for autographs and extra baseball cards. The players were always jovial and grateful."

No doubt there were some fun discussions at the signing events among the old-timers. Bobby would speak of Buck O'Neil, Satchel Paige, Jackie Robinson, Hank Aaron and countless others when he joyfully walked down memory lane with his family or friends.

Deborah chose the title "A Legend Who Walked Among Us" for the essay she shared with me about her dad. His family looks back these days and are amazed by what he accomplished. He is cherished deeply by his loved ones. At this years' opening night of the NBC Tournament, I had the honor of meeting Deborah and her family. They all proudly wore T-shirts displaying Bobby, some showing a baseball card image with "A Legend Who Walked Among Us" emblazoned across their chests.

Baseball is part of the Boyd family to this day. Bobby and his love for the game have endured through his grandsons and great-grandsons, Bryan James, Patrick James, Jordan Knox and Christian.

Bryan, who played outfield for Butler Community College and Nicholls State, said, "My grandfather had a huge influence on me playing the game of baseball. Hearing the stories of years past with him having to endure so much was one of the main contributors to me playing the game so hard; for him and his fellow peers that sacrificed so much for us in the beginning. The talks that we had about hitting, about guys' salaries before he passed are true memories I will keep forever."

Bryan graced the outfield for two National Baseball Congress Tournament teams (Wichita Braves and El Dorado Broncos). His grandfather smiled from the heavens watching Bryan connect for a base hit in the same tournament that Bobby starred in with the Dreamliners.

Patrick (catcher and right fielder in Little League) remembers his PaPa telling him to be the best that he could be on and off the field.

The next generation is now swinging bats and dreaming of home runs. Bobby's great-grandson Jordan Knox has played centerfield for Butler Community College and the University of Pine Bluff. Another great-grandson, Christian, is gracing the League 42 turf field, wearing a Diamondbacks jersey in the tee-ball division.

Sadly, Robert "Bobby" Boyd has not been recognized yet by the city of Wichita or on a larger stage by the organizations and leagues he played in. Perhaps, a story is waiting to be written on a broader scale about this man, who if alive today, could watch his six-year-old great grandson, Christian, playing League 42 tee-ball for the Diamondbacks at McAdams.

I hope you have enjoyed these stories about men who pushed through hardships and injuries, both physical and to their souls, to continue to play the game of baseball that they loved deeply. Like any romance, strength comes from managing obstacles, roadblocks and unexpected challenges along the journey of life. These men, whether Monrovians, Monarchs, Orioles or Dreamliners, were heroes to their families and communities.

4

BASEBALL'S BARNUM

DETERMINATION
Staying focused on a plan, even though the path to its end may be different.

I t is time to introduce you to Raymond Harry Dumont, a Wichita native who, in his early professional years, focused his energies and work on his love: sports. He used his passion to fuel the energy behind his pen and paper, writing sports stories for the *Wichita-Eagle Beacon* before stepping into a new role as sports editor for the *Hutchinson News.* Ray exuded a restless energy, never feeling settled or satisfied with his days in the newspaper business. Dumont ventured into the world of sporting goods, excelling as a mail-order salesperson, his tireless approach contagious to those he worked with.

Known as "Hap," a nickname coined by those who marveled at his nonstop positive energy, Dumont was never seen without a cigar clenched between two fingers, tobacco leaves artistically woven into an article of enjoyment that Hap chewed on through the day, casting it aside for a new one once the cigar had resigned itself to damply unraveling. His talents for marketing translated into the early days of promoting local boxing and wrestling matches, drawing crowds to sports that were limited to smaller audiences than his favorite sport, baseball.

By his late twenties, Dumont's restlessness and thirst for marketing merged, exemplified by his ingenious promotion of a game of baseball between circus clowns and firefighters. This is not a typo! How did Hap pull off a game that drew a sellout crowd of 3,500 fans to Island Park on Ackerman Island? He knew that in the state of Kansas, the blue laws prevented specific business activities, including the circus, but not the game of baseball on Sundays. The men who brought the world of clowns alive the other six days of the week wanted to earn money on Sundays, voicing interest in squaring off against a local baseball team. The idea came to Hap: Why not put a baseball game together with the clowns versus a local club of firefighters?

Dumont had a knack for unearthing gimmicks and surprises that would thrill the spectators. In one dugout, Dumont had the Sparks Brothers Circus clowns, eager to entertain, led by Abe Goldstein, a twenty-nine-year-old clown who captivated Americans from coast to coast as one of the Keystone Kops. Goldstein had developed his showtime routine by then. He would appear as Korkey the Komic Kop, wearing a baggy and worn coat with brass buttons, swinging a flexible baton from his right hand. I am not sure how Korkey was able to play ball at Island Park, considering his penchant for comically tormenting his "Teddys," mutts trained to fall dead as he emptied his toy gun at them driving the Teddy's to grasp his rear end. As the Komic Kop transitioned between innings, leaving his bat in the dugout and hopping into the stands buzzing with laughter, the centerfielder for the firemen's team took his position on the back of a motorcycle that patrolled the expansive grass, driven by a Wichita police officer. This was not a normal baseball game!

Success in 1925 served as a springboard for Hap's new idea of introducing a state semiprofessional baseball tournament in his hometown of Wichita. By 1931, the ideas had crystallized into the creation of the Kansas State Baseball Tournament. Hap landed the tournament on Ackerman Island in the same ballpark that was the stage for the Wichita Monrovians in their historic showdown with the No. 6 Ku Klux Klan team in 1923, as well as his compelling draw two years later, pitting America's clowns against Wichita's finest firefighters.

Four years later, Hap, cigar in hand and dressed in an impeccable charcoal striped suit, founded the National Semi-Pro Baseball Congress, an organization that evolved from the state tournament.[23] Dumont was recognized by fans in the state of Kansas but had not stepped onto the national stage yet. His relentless drive and innovation led to an epiphany: Hap needed a big-name baseball player for the inaugural World Series to elevate the new tournament.

Stage right, the curtain was pulled back, and out stepped Satchel Paige and his Bismarck Churchills barnstorming team! Satchel agreed to bring the integrated team to Wichita, motivated by Dumont's guarantee of a

Hap Dumont, the founder of the National Baseball Congress. *Courtesy of the National Baseball Congress and Katie Woods.*

$1,000 personal appearance fee. As was so common in the days of barnstorming baseball, the team piled into two cars (a Chrysler Airflow and a Plymouth sedan) supplied by team owner Neil Churchill, who owned a car dealership in Bismarck, North Dakota.

The front-opening rear doors were a blessing for the guys on the team, as they made it easier for a crowd of long-legged young men to jam into every inch of open space as they trekked southeast toward Wichita. The Churchills earned gas and food money by playing games in towns along the way. I cannot imagine how stifling it was for the guys crammed into these two cars, with gear, clothes and food all squeezed into the confines of both cars, windows down to push the heavy air through as miles passed.

Tom Dunkel, the author of *Color Blind: The Forgotten Team that Broke Baseball's Color Line*, discussed the power of Paige as a drawing card for the first tournament. Fans flocked to the grandstands for all four of Satchel's starts, almost doubling the attendance.

Hap had taken a huge risk; promising Satchel $1,000 that Dumont did not have. Hap, with a cigar clenched tightly in his fingers and his head covered by his trademark hat, was gambling that the gate receipts would more than cover Paige's pay.

The National Semi-Pro Baseball Congress sprinted out of the gate with their inaugural World Series. Dumont not only secured one of the greatest pitchers ever to play in the tournament, but he also landed thirty-one additional teams to play over sixteen days under a stifling sun and whipping southern winds in Wichita.

Dumont was a risk taker. In the inaugural tournament, he took a bold approach to building out the roster of teams, integrating the series with other "colored" teams, including a Native team from Wewoka, Oklahoma; a Japanese American team from Stockton, California; and four other Black teams.

Dunkel highlighted that what happened in Wichita in the inaugural tournament caught Branch Rickey's attention, who, at the time, was the general manager of the St. Louis Cardinals. Rickey was watching how people would react to an integrated team. Dunkel said, "So that tournament, I think, definitely raised both Paige's profile and opened the door to the possibility of the Major Leagues being integrated."[24]

Commissioner Judge Kennesaw Mountain Landis and Major League Baseball anticipated that this unexpected pool of talented ballplayers would yield substantial benefits for the league. The tournament could serve as their "minor league," saving the organizations money that they didn't have to spend developing players. Landis encouraged club scouts to head to Wichita to sign the best of the best.

Fans packed the stands at the newest park in Wichita, Lawrence Stadium, that the city had built after the 1933 fire had leveled Island Park, the rickety, wooden grandstand ballpark that had been home to the Kansas State Tournaments. The cost to get into the games ranged from $0.40 to a staggering $1.10.

Baseball spectators were entertained over the two weeks of the series, fortunate to witness Satchel Paige strike out sixty batters in four starts as the Bismarck Churchills claimed the first championship in the history of the National Baseball Congress. His team knocked off the Halliburton Cementers of Duncan, Oklahoma, pulling in $2,500 for winning the title. He struck out fourteen and drove a run in with a single in the final game.

Satchel Paige and the 1935 Bismarck Churchills. *Courtesy of NBC and Katie Woods.*

Satchel was named the first MVP for his efforts; amazingly, his strikeout record still stands today, in the ninetieth year of the National Baseball Congress World Series Tournament.

The first year catapulted the NBC onto the national stage. Dumont's innovative approach flourished in the years to come. Unfortunately, due to pressures from Major League Baseball and their opposition to integration, the NBC did not select minority teams to participate for over a decade, until Jackie Robinson and the Dodgers broke the color barrier. The drastic change, so quickly implemented after the first year, left a mark of disgrace on the NBC (as well as the MLB), preventing great ballplayers, with different colored skin and big dreams, of having the opportunity to shine on the yearly World Series stage in front of pro scouts.

He introduced innovations to the game that were so advanced, they cast a shadow over future decades and other pioneers, including Bill Veeck and Charlie O. Finley.

Be amazed at the list of innovations that Ray "Hap" Dumont implemented:

1. He had an underground microphone designed to be positioned behind home plate.[25] At the prompt of the umpire, the microphone would rise, locking in place, allowing the umpire to announce lineup changes. Comically, umpire arguments with players and coaches were picked up by the microphone, casting colorful words across the stands—some words too strong for the little ones enjoying their popcorn!

2. Umpires also had an innovation literally at their feet behind the plate. An automatic plate duster, designed by a local company, Cardwell Manufacturing, would clean home plate with a burst of compressed air. All the umpire had to do was step on a plate in the dirt.[26]

3. A few gimmicks tended to be short-lived, including early sunrise morning games to catch the graveyard shift workers with the offer of free coffee and/or donuts, as well as free admission to any spectators that came sporting their pajamas!

4. In 1940, Hap introduced the first semblance of a designated hitter to the NBC. The elimination of the weak-hitting pitchers from the lineup could now be addressed with the use of a pinch hitter. By 1941, tournaments were utilizing the "designated hitter" rule, successful in its implementation and welcomed by the fans.[27] Thirty-two years later, I watched Luis Tiant face Ron

Blomberg of the Yankees in the April season-opener, a first-time MLB duel between a pitcher and DH!

5. Hap introduced a time clock. The clock would start ticking when the pitcher received the ball from the catcher, requiring that the pitcher let one fly within twenty seconds. Breaking the new rule resulted in a ball being awarded to the batter.[28] Dumont's motivation was fueled by increasing gate receipts through reducing time between pitches, speeding up games and opening the door to more games played each day during the tournament. Brilliant, innovative and ahead of its time. Decades later, the MLB introduced time clock rules and regulations at the outset of the 2022 season.

6. Dumont pushed into uncharted territory in the world of umpiring, introducing Luther "Dummy" Taylor during World War II as his first deaf umpire. Taylor, who utilized sign language during his days as a starting pitcher for John McGraw and the New York Giants, to call the games. Hap also introduced the first female umpire during the 1943 NBC tournament. Lorraine Heinisch worked the bases for two games, receiving high marks for her efforts.[29] In Hap's estimation, the first "wump," was a success. This move coincided with the start of the All-American Girls Professional Baseball League that same summer. Unfortunately, this barrier-breaking venture hasn't spread into the MLB as of this writing, which is very disappointing.

7. Other innovations did, at times, fail for Dumont and the National Baseball Congress. The first failure was his attempt to play night games more effectively, without lights, built on the premise that orange baseballs, plus glow-in-the-dark paint applied to gloves, caps, bases, bats and all chalk lines would be a way to conserve energy for the war effort. The ghost-like apparitions stumbled on the field with this short-lived concept!

8. One of his craziest ideas, put into play for just one game—which I wish I had the opportunity to watch—was a rule built on the premise of creating pure chaos on the basepaths. Where should a spectator look during a game when a batter, striking a grounder through the infield, had the choice of running to first *or* third (if the base was open)? This idea, introduced in an exhibition game in 1944, drove a lifelong memory for the lucky spectators, who watched two runners score at the same

time, stealing home from first and third, paralyzing the catcher sandwiched between the baserunners coming down both lines!

Hap Dumont was the king of innovation during the middle of the twentieth century. Bill Veeck brought that same talent to MLB in his day, rivaling Dumont for the title of the "Barnum of Baseball."

Dumont worked every day of the year at the helm of the NBC, arriving at the offices via a cab or through the good graces of work associates because of his decision to not own a car. His tireless efforts continued to push his yearly tournament onto the national stage; the balding, diminutive baseball genius was ever-present in the offices and on the ball field during series time. He was always in his suit, with a seasoned wide-brimmed hat, squeezing the life out of the unlit, heavily chewed cigar.

This amazing man continued to push change within the NBC. In the 1960s, "Semi-Pro" was dropped from the league's name, as an increase in the number of college baseball players in the tournament came into play. Think about the trajectory the National Baseball Congress had taken since its inaugural World Series, starting with the ageless Satchel Paige in 1935.

The yearly tournament, held in the hottest span of the summer, between late July and mid-August, was now playing host to summer ball clubs with rosters of talented college ballplayers, who would come to Wichita from locations ranging from Alaska (Goldpanners from Fairbanks) to Santa Barbara (Foresters) and Fort Wayne (Voltmen). When I visited the Wichita Baseball Museum, my baseball knowledge was shaken as I learned for the first time about the more than three hundred alumni who played in Major League Baseball. Stars such as Ron Guidry, Tom Seaver, Joe Carter, Mark McGwire, Barry Bonds, Nolan Ryan, Randy Johnson and Dave Winfield had career paths that stopped in Wichita prior to their days in Major League Baseball.

Dumont's innovations included an umpire's microphone to announce lineup changes. *Courtesy of the Wichita Baseball Museum.*

Hap, fueled by an amazing work ethic, had a *determination* to continue to push innovation and growth through a

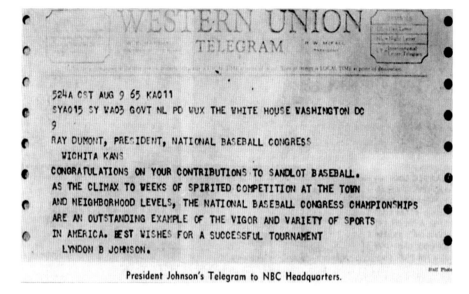

524A CST AUG 9 65 KA011
SYA015 SY WA03 GOVT NL PD WUX THE WHITE HOUSE WASHINGTON DC
9
RAY DUMONT, PRESIDENT, NATIONAL BASEBALL CONGRESS
    WICHITA KANS
CONGRATULATIONS ON YOUR CONTRIBUTIONS TO SANDLOT BASEBALL.
AS THE CLIMAX TO WEEKS OF SPIRITED COMPETITION AT THE TOWN
AND NEIGHBORHOOD LEVELS, THE NATIONAL BASEBALL CONGRESS CHAMPIONSHIPS
ARE AN OUTSTANDING EXAMPLE OF THE VIGOR AND VARIETY OF SPORTS
IN AMERICA. BEST WISHES FOR A SUCCESSFUL TOURNAMENT
    LYNDON B JOHNSON.

President Johnson's Telegram to NBC Headquarters.

President Lyndon B. Johnson's 1965 telegram to Ray Dumont, NBC. *Courtesy of the Wichita Eagle.*

quarter of a century. He stood proudly within the baseball world, cognizant of how his innovation influenced great baseball in Wichita and served as a catalyst for change on the big-league stage.

The 1971 tournament would unfold without the presence of Ray "Hap" Dumont on the ball field or in the stands. Dumont died suddenly of a heart attack in his office at Lawrence-Dumont Stadium just weeks before the tournament was to start. Hap had been working at his desk that day, trying to secure Joe Garagiola to make a tournament appearance that summer.

Fifty-three years have passed since baseball lost a great innovator. Dumont had not laid out instructions on how the league should continue after his death. His widow decided to sell the tournament and organization. Through the decades, its stewardship has passed from leader to leader. An organization that had thrived for close to four decades under the leadership of one man found itself surviving but not necessarily thriving through the following decades.

Larry Davis, a onetime president of the NBC, talked about the challenge of filling the innovative void within the tournament's organization, sharing, "To many, Dumont was the National Baseball Congress. Some of the NBC died with him in July of 1971."

There is no doubt that the NBC struggled to refine its identity in the early decades after Dumont passed.

The City of Wichita took ownership of the National Baseball Congress, transitioning it from a for-profit organization to the new nonprofit National Baseball Congress Foundation. The city understood at the time the power of the legacy that was started in 1935 and its importance to the greater Wichita community.

The foundation recognized that change in the baseball world is reshaping how they need to look at what the definition of success is for the National Baseball Congress tournament in the coming years. Part of their success will be realized through their mission to "grow and popularize the NBC World Series as the premier summer showcase for the best baseball players in the world." The foundation's focus was on setting the stage for great summer college teams to compete against the best, while continuing to delight and entertain the next generation of fans who buy in to the tournament as an experience that will be remembered for a lifetime and not just a bunch of games.

Hap's determination to forge a path for his National Baseball Congress to become integral in the world of baseball has paid off for close to ninety years. I have no doubt that Ray "Hap" Dumont is happy today as he looks at the foundation's community outreach efforts and its newfound focus on celebrating the sport's history in relevant ways, such as welcoming back Satchel's family to the ninetieth anniversary tournament this summer.

On the opening night of the 2024 World Series, Satchel's grandson Michael spoke to an audience about Paige's legacy both on and off the field. Michael's granddad helped to put the National Baseball Congress on the national map in 1935. Odds are that if the first tournament had been a bust, Hap's dream could have fallen flat.

Michael shared that the celebration in 2024, accentuated by a Satchel bobblehead giveaway, "Is credit and honor that is long deserved." Michael shared that his granddad's legacy was "his longevity," as he had pitched for close to forty years with nary an injury. Satchel understood what his link to Hap and the NBC meant for his long and storied career.

Stay tuned for more information about the National Baseball Congress Foundation in several chapters that celebrate the first woman NBC Tournament director and what she and her team strive to accomplish in the future as they begin operating independently in 2025.

405 SOUTH TENTH STREET

COURAGE
Doing what you know is the right thing, even when it is hard to do.

About all we did, other than play baseball, was go to the movies.[30]
—Bob Mallon, Independence Yankee teammate and roommate

Courage was an important word in Mickey Mantle's vocabulary, because his dad and hero, Mutt, was nothing but courageous. The definition of *courage* is "the ability to do something that frightens one and/or strength in the face of pain and grief." What unfolds in this chapter is the story of Mickey in his early professional days, playing for the Independence Yankees and facing what appeared to be insurmountable challenges to this quiet, anxious seventeen-year-old ballplayer.

Before I get to the story, I want to bring courage into play and share a personal story with you. I have a memory of my early high school days in a new state, a new town and a new school that shaped a character flaw in my first months as a sixteen-year-old. I was quiet, anxious and lonely as I walked the hallways of this new school in a fog, burying myself in getting As, struggling to make new friends and isolating myself in our new home six miles outside of town.

I decided to try out for the high school basketball team early in the fall of 1976. I cannot remember much about the tryouts outside of the panic I felt while changing in a locker room where everyone knew each other, feeling as if

I was on an island. After surviving charging drills, my next memory is of the day I found out whether I had made the team. I surreptitiously found my way to the painted concrete wall to the left of the gym doors, where the coach had posted the upcoming season's roster. My eyes darted down the page, coming to an abrupt stop at a line that said "Mike Travis." I had made the team!

The indelible mark is still within me, because I decided to run, to not report to practice and leave behind all that had transpired on the basketball court marked by my Nike basketball sneakers. I did not have the courage to report to the first practice. Taking the comfortable versus the courageous route impacted me for decades—until I finally developed the courage I did not have as a youngster through my professional career, inspired by my wife, Ivy, a strong, courageous woman.

So, as I look down at my left inside forearm and read the tattoo that serves as a daily reminder, "Le courage over le confort," I know that now is the time to talk about seventeen-year-old Mickey Mantle, his days playing minor-league ball in Independence, Kansas, and how Major League Baseball came so close to never knowing no. 7, the future Hall of Famer.

Hardscrabble Commerce, Oklahoma, is where the story starts. Mickey and his four younger siblings shared a bed in his childhood home, surrounded by coal mining families, the mines, the ubiquitous coal dust and tempting alkali fields that became ballparks when the boys wanted to play a game. The dust, permeating the floorboards in their homes and finding its way intrusively into everyone's eyes, nose and mouth did not stop the boys from playing ballgames in their early years.

Mickey was intent on playing infield, thus his first professional position, shortstop. This stemmed from a desire to avoid the endless running the guys in the outfield had to do when a gapper hit on an alkali field would roll on forever, traveling on top of yards of lead and zinc. As he manned his position, dreaming about his next at-bat and the long fly he would launch, dust would spring from the ground as he moved—he was the vision of Pig-Pen, and his inherent permanent cloud of dust in *The Peanuts*.

That same dust was floating in the air deep below ground, coating Mutt Mantle as he toiled away each day, anxious to see the surface of Commerce after nine hours of working at one of the Eagle-Picher mines that marred the surrounding landscape. No matter how beaten-down Mutt was, he and Mickey would head to the backyard to work on Mantle's switch-hitting progress. His bat was often a broomstick, and the balls that flew to the plate were beaten-down tennis balls, losing life as Mickey's bat pounded the spheres. The work was hard, the atmosphere aggressive, as Mutt threw pitch after pitch toward his son, their leaning shed accepting the role of backstop. Groundouts were death to Mickey, each one registering as an out. Mickey would get into his stance, praying that he could at least hit the house on the fly and knowing that the liners smacking the clapboards below the windows were doubles.

Mickey would pepper the lower half of the house, hitting from the right side with greater frequency and establishing himself as a better hitter on average from that side. He smiled inwardly when he launched the occasional triple above the window, feet from the roof. As Mutt worked him unceasingly to become a strong switch-hitter, he was struck by the power his son exhibited from the left side of the plate, looking up to the sky painted with sunset streaks and watching the distant ball soar over their house for another home run. Little did either of them know—let alone dream—that just under 70 percent of Mickey's 536 career home runs would be launched from the left side of the plate.

As Mickey's graduation day approached, he knew that he would be absent, naturally prioritizing playing for the Baxter Whiz Kids. The folks in Commerce, including Mutt, Mickey and the family, knew that graduation day meant Mantle could sign his first professional contract. Little did they know that Lee McPhail with the Yankees was pressuring a local scout for the pinstripes to sign Mantle. What stood in the way was a game in which Mickey went 4 for 5, homering right-handed and thumping a double and two singles left-handed. Tom Greenwood ushered Mutt and Mickey into his car, the roof above them holding back hard rains, as Mickey signed a contract (Mutt had to sign said contract as a parental guardian since Mickey was still seventeen) with orders to report to Independence.

The Commerce newspaper, the *Commerce News-Post*, shared a front-page news story, "Mickey Mantle Signs with Yankees," on June 9, 1949.

> *Mickey Mantle, a former Picher sandlotter of the old Gabby Street League days and a graduate of the Commerce high school, has been signed by a New York Yankee base ball* [sic] *club to a contract....Playing with the Whiz Kids last year, Mantle batted .431 for the summer against some of the best amateur pitchers in the district. No terms were announced, and it is not known whether he received a bonus or not.*

Three landmarks became Mickey's home away from home as he settled into a new life just over seventy miles away from his childhood home, a grim mining community and his dad's hope for his son. Shulthis Stadium, the local movie theater and 405 South Tenth Street were his baseball beacons.

Shulthis Stadium, a wonderful park that was built in the early 1900s, had a classic brick grandstand that became one of the oldest grandstands in the United States, built in the same generation as Fenway and Wrigley. Mantle would dig into the batter's box and peer out at the wooden fence that hid the sight of Monkey Island, a favorite zoo exhibit, but it was not able to keep the sounds of the residents of said island—yes, monkeys—from being heard as they asked Mickey to launch one their way, over the centerfield fence.

At seventeen, Mickey shared a twin bed in a boardinghouse with Bob Mallon, another Yankee who dreamed of stepping on the mound in the Bronx someday. When not playing ball, the two opted to catch the latest film with great frequency.

This is where the theme of courage versus comfort comes into play. Mickey was homesick, and this was exacerbated by his early struggles as a minor leaguer. He played his first professional game as shortstop, batting seventh, on June 14, 1949. The *Independence Record*, the local newspaper, stated, "Mickey Mantle, newest addition to the Yank roster, hit two for four and fielded his position errorlessly." His hometown paper, the *Commerce News-Post*, shared the following with their readers.

His false hopes after hitting in the first three games came crashing down in his fourth start, a game in which Mickey went hitless and showed his defensive liabilities, making three errors.

The young ballplayer was a nervous wreck, and he wondered if he could make it long enough as a Yankee to collect the larger portion of his bonus check. One night, as he and Bob were hanging out in their room, hours after his roommate's first win as a starter, Mickey asked him if he wanted him to sign the game ball Bob was tossing and catching. Mallon responded, "Why would I want your autograph?"[31]

His defensive woes continued to mount, errors showing up in the box

---

Mick Mantle Breaks Up Ball Game in Mi-ami Monday Evening

Micky Mantle the Commerce boy who is having his first tryout in organized baseball, playing with the Independence, Kansas team in the KMO league, broke up the ball game in Miami Monday night when he rapped a double against the score board in deep right field with the bases loaded. Mantle was making his first appearance before his home town fans who had assembled to watch him play against Miami and he gave the home boys something to talk about, both by his fielding plays as well as his batting prowess. From all appearances Monday evening, Mantle is on his way up the baseball ladder.

Mickey Mantle, early season action in the press. *Courtesy of the* Commerce News-Post.

score almost every game. Charlie Weber, his double play partner, shared years later, "Mick was the worst shortstop I ever played alongside. He would almost kill you."[32] Mickey would peg balls resembling Mahomes bullets from short distances to Charlie, who was dancing toward the second base bag, hopeful of turning two or at least a force out. Mantle's arm was a missile, but his aim fell short, and his throws sailed over first base.

I stood on the sidewalk in front of 405 South Tenth Street, looking at a dandelion-filled empty lot. I was not disappointed at the site, because I could feel the pain Mickey had to stomach as his dad laid into him about calling it quits. Mickey was doubting his abilities to make it and had called his dad in Commerce, stating that he wanted to come home. Mickey was worried, thinking about how much his dad sacrificed for him to make it to the big leagues. "It looked like I wasn't going to do it," Mickey shared later in life. Imagine Mutt receiving that call and digesting what his son was saying. Mutt's mining days were no doubt going to shorten his life, as they had for his dad and granddad.

I can understand why Mutt would have had an issue with Mickey's phone call. The life of a miner was brutal. Death could arrive any day in the mines. Lives were shortened through the daily consumption of coal dust. On top of that, in the summer of 1949, the Eagle-Picher mine owners had shut down the mines for close to five weeks due to a disagreement over contract negotiations. Several weeks after Mutt drove to Independence to counsel his son, mining news was splashed on the front cover of the town paper. The *Commerce News-Post* broke the news on August 11, 1949, that the mines were soon to reopen. The miners lost the battle with the new contract, which stipulated workers would return with a painful cut in hourly pay. The grind became even more exhausting as families tried to make do with less income, realizing that what Eagle-Picher dangled out there: "a guarantee of a sliding wage based upon the price of zinc", was not a certainty.

Life was hard, grinding and defeating, yet Mutt felt a glimmer of hope that Mickey could represent the first break in a tragic Mantle tradition of working underground and dying young. Mutt drove those seventy miles north, thinking about this opportunity his son had. He was disconsolate about his world, his anger and disbelief building that Mickey wanted to come home.

Mutt made it clear that if Mickey was a coward, a quitter, then he had best pack his belongings up and come back to work a life in the mines. Mickey's dad questioned him: "Do you want to go back into those damn mines?" Mantle's siblings were tucked together on the porch of the boardinghouse as their dad hit their brother with verbal uppercuts. The brutal talk, the endless family life without love and empathy present, put the fear of failure in Mickey, who decided overnight that sticking it out and playing ball was what he had to do.

His roommate penned a letter to his parents on July 26, telling them, "I room with Mantle, the shortstop. He was hitting .230 a week and a half ago, he went on a hitting streak and jumped up to .300 in that time. He's as fast as lightning, beats out a lot of infield hits and bunts."[33] Bob had captured a glimpse of the transformation in Mickey's ability to hit at this level. Confidence grew in the seventeen-year-old as he took a four-game streak of 12 for 17 and stretched it to 16 for 24 over six games. Mantle was tearing up pitching, driving his batting average up by 71 points! No doubt, Mickey had found a groove and a newfound confidence that he belonged. Mantle did not show his power quite yet, hitting just 7 home runs for the year.

Tall tales are always present in sports, such as with a golfer sharing a story of a near hole-in-one. These same traits can boost a decent home run into a tape measure monster. This is where Monkey Island, located maybe fifty feet beyond the center field wall, comes into play.

Monkey Island, situated beyond the centerfield fence at the historic Shulthis Stadium in Independence. *Author's collection.*

One long ball Mickey hit out of his home park is said to have landed on Monkey Island, bouncing off the limestone walls that were home to monkeys and no doubt eventually falling into the moat, popping to the surface and doing a backstroke.

The year ended, and Mickey finished with an average of .322, hitting seven homers and driving in sixty-eight runs. Mantle's hometown paper once again gave him front-page billing (in a paper that consisted of four pages), closing the recap of his first year in pro ball, stating, "With this brand of ball playing, young Mantle, no doubt is headed for the big time. Congratulations, Mickey."[34]

He would be haunted through the winter, recoiling from the memories of making close to fifty errors, which would continue to drag down his defensive play in the next year of minor-league ball.

Let us pause for a moment and reflect on Mickey's mortal battle between courage and comfort. Whereas I, the author (and no big-league ballplayer), ran toward comfort at the expense of growing a stronger backbone, Mickey sucked it up and pushed on. If it were not for the hardscrabble life in Commerce, the awe with which he looked up to his dad and the firsthand knowledge of the gruesomeness working in the mines could inflict, Mickey could have folded and headed seventy miles south to a tough life. There might have been no number 7 in New York, no majestic home runs, no Mantle smile vying with the dazzling lights of Broadway for fans in New York City.

Mantle went on to have a stellar second season, despite 55 errors at shortstop, hitting .383 with 26 home runs, 136 RBIs, 141 runs scored and capturing the MVP award while wearing the Joplin Miners uniform. Mickey was invited to join the Yankees at spring training in 1951.

I want to share a classic story from his first spring training with the Yankees. In an exhibition game out west, leading into the regular season, Mickey launched two massive 500-foot home runs. One of his two left-handed behemoths was rumored to have traveled close to 600 feet after clearing the 439-foot-tall centerfield wall, eventually landing on the practice field of the mighty USC Trojan football team. An offensive huddle was interrupted moments later, when the ball rolled into the middle of the Trojans, bouncing off Frank Gifford's foot![35]

Drop the mic, Mickey.

The story from then on is one we baseball fans know well. Mickey went on to a Hall of Fame career, despite suffering a tragic knee injury in the 1951 World Series. At one point, early in the season, Mickey dialed the rotary phone again, connecting with his dad and questioning if he could make it after Casey Stengel sent Mickey down to the Triple A Kansas City Blues to work on making better contact. Mickey felt like he was done. Sudden courage surfaced after another visit from Mutt. The rest is history.

"I FEEL LIKE I STEPPED ONTO ANOTHER PLANET"

Alex Hugo, captain and second baseman
on the USA Women's National Baseball Team.

TEAMWORK
Working with other people toward a common goal.

COURAGE
Doing what you know is the right thing, even when it is hard to do.

*C*ourage is underscored in this chapter by three trailblazers who have impacted baseball in their own unique ways. Think back to the horrors that citizens of the United States were witnessing in their hometowns during World War II. Desperate for the latest war news, people stayed up late, huddled around the family radio or the local newspaper with ink-stained fingers. Place yourself in Hutchinson, Kansas, back in 1942. The front-page headlines were overwhelming, even for myself, eight decades later as I scanned the *Hutchinson News*, with a state of exhaustion settling in as I read fourteen months of daily papers, spilling into the late spring of 1943.

Bold print in large font and photographs in black and white jumped at me as they communicated tragedy, horror and death through their pixels. As I scanned the daily pages of this small-town newspaper, I observed that the death notices covered more real estate as the months passed, balanced by the paper's stories of an increase in the number of young men called to duty.

Sports figures were struggling to understand the role they played in the lives of Americans. More men were called to duty—from local diamond heroes to billboard stars such as Joe DiMaggio, Ted Williams and Bob Feller. The winter of 1942 brought national unrest and uncertainty to life at home, life at war and the life of the game Americans loved: baseball.

Wartime baseball continued to be played, with major changes in how far teams would travel to play (due to fuel shortages and cost), how rosters were composed (with many players signing up to fight for their country) and how many fans had the energy, money or time to watch a ball game from the stands.

One team owner, Philip Knight Wrigley, who was loyal to his Cubs while he balanced his efforts with the family chewing gum business, decided to step out with a new venture for baseball fans. Wrigley put $100,000 behind the organization of a glamor league, called the All-American Girls Professional Softball League. AP wire stories capturing this news found their way from big city newspaper print to small-town America newspapers in the Midwest, including the *Hutchinson News*.[36]

Our first trailblazer, Joyce Barnes, a high school student in Hutchinson, had no idea what was happening in Chicago. Joyce, born on a farm just south of Hutchinson, spent many free hours playing with whatever she, her two older brothers and her younger sister could scrounge up from the dust around their home. Her parents, Edward and Ethel, were happy to see the children distracted from the hardship of managing a farm and the local headlines dropped on the front page of their paper through the pursuit of childhood happiness evolving around ballgames of any kind.

Joyce, who I watched in a 2009 interview, struck me as someone I wish I could have met.[37] I listened to a vibrant older woman, her head framed by curly hair and her face painted with smile wrinkles, share her stories with an understated, soft, warm laugh.

Always one of the tallest kids in the small town, Joyce did not play ball with a glove until she entered grade school. "We were happy, and we played ball," she said, smiling at memories of everyone chasing the batted ball, bare feet stirring up dust, grasshoppers and pure joy.

In sixth grade, her teacher in their country school decided that Joyce would be their pitcher. Journeys to play other teams in neighboring towns unfolded over those years. Joyce shared her love for sports during the interview, reminiscing about her softball and basketball memories. Life was different for women in the 1940s. When she entered high school, she was not allowed to compete as she had in her earlier, carefree days, because the general mindset was that playing ball was too strenuous for girls.

Saturdays in her farmhouse were full of chores, kids being kids when they created moments of idle time. Something drew Joyce to the latest *News* edition that ushered in May 1943, laying lifeless on the kitchen table. There's no doubt she quietly digested the front-page headlines of horror and loss, rushing to page two to read more slowly the latest news in sports, both local and national in scope. Joyce, missing the structured ballgames that she dominated as a pitcher, spotted a headline above the fold in the second to far-right column, titled "Glamor Girls for Softball," with a subtitle powerful in its simplicity, "National League Formed by Wrigley."[38]

Joyce, all of seventeen years old and closing in on the completion of her junior year in high school, swallowed the rest of the story in a rush, her head spinning at the possibilities taking shape. The AP story out of Chicago shared that Philip K. Wrigley, the owner of the Cubs, had sent talent scouts to "hunt down beauty as well as playing ability." At that point, trials had been held in more than ten Midwestern and Southwestern cities, with the search spreading as far as our northern neighbor, Canada.

Glamor Girls For Softball

National League Formed By Wrigley

Chicago (AP)—Philip K. Wrigley, owner of the Chicago Cubs, has peeled off $100,000 to organize a glamor circuit called the All-American Girls Softball league.

He has sent talent scouts to hunt down beauty as well as playing ability. Trials have been held in at least 10 midwestern and southwestern cities, and the search has reached as far as Canada to sign players for salaries ranging from $50 to $80 a week.

Upwards of 100 girls will report at Chicago's Wrigley field May 17 for spring training and will get paid for it. Sixty will be selected, 15 going to each of the four teams in the league. A 100-game schedule, including many exhibitions at navy and army bases, will start May 30.

Racine and Kenosha in Wisconsin already have been selected as league members.

"The league is a non-profit venture," explained Wrigley. "Proceeds will be used to expand. We eventually hope to build a structure of minor leagues. The league itself will control the players, rather than the clubs, to maintain a balance of talent assuring close competition."

Revolutionary softball rules have been adopted to speed up play, and each team will have its girls arrayed in pink, blue, green or yellow uniforms with three-quarter-length flair skirts.

Glamor Girls needed. *Courtesy of the Hutchinson News.*

Joyce could not believe that these girls would be paid salaries ranging from fifty to eighty dollars per week to play softball. She continued to read, oblivious to the swirling energy of her siblings around her and found that close to one hundred girls would be reporting to Wrigley Field on May 17, just sixteen days later, for spring training.

The AAGPSL (All-American Girls Professional Softball League) had initially selected the communities of Racine and Kenosha for its teams' home bases. Wrigley shared other details in this six-paragraph story, including that four teams would be formed for the first year of play in 1943, with sixty girls filling those rosters.

Wrigley stated, "The league is a non-profit venture. Proceeds will be used to expand. We eventually hope to build a structure of minor leagues. The league itself will control the players, rather than the clubs, to maintain a balance of talent assuring close competition."[39]

Joyce released the sports page from her damp hands, sweaty with excitement, thinking about how she wanted to try out for this league, glossing over the closing comments in the article that "each team will have its girls arrayed in pink, blue, green or yellow uniforms with three-quarter-length flared skirts."[40]

Statuesque at seventeen and confident in herself and her athletic abilities, Joyce decided her next step was to write a letter to Mr. Wrigley, stating that she wanted an opportunity to try out for the league. Our postal service, with its stellar reputation and expedient movement of letters, ushered her letter to his desk in just days. She ripped open the response from Wrigley, finding a train ticket for one to come up to the windy city in time for the May 17 tryouts.

Her mom stepped in and said that she would not allow Joyce to travel alone on a train. Joyce wrote a second letter to Wrigley, requesting that her mom be able to travel with her so she could try out. The response was to the point, stating that of course her mom could join her for the journey, but they would not pay her expenses.

Joyce demonstrated courage in everything she did to make this trek possible. When they arrived, this young woman, who had played short field in grade school because of her strong arm and speed, had the opportunity to try out. Meanwhile, Ethel met the coach and team chaperone and "decided that she was safe," and she soon departed for Hutchinson, leaving her daughter behind.[41]

I wish I could speak about the lengthy career that Joyce had—but I cannot.

Her time with the Kenosha Comets was short-lived. Joyce was handed her green outfit and shoes. "I was there for three weeks, and they paid me forty dollars while I was there." This courageous young woman experienced several firsts in her life. She donned the Comets glamor uniform, fans calling the team the Shamrocks due to the green uniform as they took the field. Joyce learned, along with her teammates, about proper etiquette, makeup application and hair styling from the team chaperone, who was responsible for the safety of the team of fifteen girls. Their chaperone carried the burden to make sure that the girls hit the field fitting the bill, glamorous and athletic.

Her playing time was limited to pitching just in practices and riding the pine in the dugouts in Kenosha, Racine, Rockford and South Bend. Her roommate during her time with the Comets, Audrey Wagner, became one of the best hitters in league history, fueling a pennant-winning inaugural season for the Comets with forty-three runs batted in.[42]

Joyce did not have the opportunity to pitch in a game or celebrate the pennant; her new experiences while she was teammate to the other girls included a venture to a beer joint, where, laughingly, Joyce remembers that "it wasn't a very good one," adding that she got sick from the escapades.

One of the sixty founding members in the inaugural season of the AAGPBL, Joyce left the team with a return ticket paid for by Wrigley,

Above: Introducing the Kenosha Comets. *Courtesy of the* Kenosha News.

Opposite: All-American Girls Professional Baseball League logo. *Courtesy of Wikipedia.*

eventually landing back at home in Hutchinson during the summer before she went on to finish her high school years, graduating in 1944. Joyce played four sports as her last year of school flew by, including basketball, volleyball, track and field and, of course, softball.

The AAGPBL lives on through those remaining "girls," who today are celebrated for their accomplishments. Joyce was one of many players who had the opportunity to be in the movie *A League of Their Own*. After the movie's release, she couldn't help but feel like an icon.

The creation of this league of women ballplayers, created by Wrigley, was a game-changer in American life. Wrigley and League President Ken Sells believed that femininity was the key factor in building a league set to provide entertainment in small midwestern towns that were going through significant changes, witnessing factories just down the street shift to war production efforts. These women, their ages ranging from fifteen to twenty-five, typically came from working-class or rural families, knowing that they could earn more playing ball than they could in factory jobs or traditional secretarial work.

Joyce seized her opportunity in 1943. Her courage opened a door to an experience that only a privileged few had known. This young woman, our first trailblazer to be highlighted in this chapter, tosses both a softball and a baseball to another groundbreaker, Alex Hugo, later in the chapter. The story of Alex Hugo must wait though. Let us revisit the National Baseball Congress (chapter 4), founded by Hap Dumont, a league built on innovation, a landmark institution that lost the transformational magic in the decades following Dumont's death.

Meet Katie Crawford Woods, who grew up in a sports family. Her dad was a basketball coach; her extended family has a collection of football, baseball and additional basketball coaches. Growing up around coaches, Katie recognized at an early age the impact sports had on communities, families and athletes far beyond the action on the field.

What I love about Katie's story is that her journey emanates from her love of sports, manifesting itself in newfound organizational opportunities. The first magical step was a four-month-long internship with the Houston Astros as the community relations intern. This introduction, thanks to a phone call and offer from the Astros, served as a springboard for a young woman with big aspirations.

Her next stop was Everett, Washington. The early community relations experience opened doors for her with the Everett AquaSox. This minor-league team, playing in the short-season Class A Northwest League, is an affiliate of the Seattle Mariners. Katie built a strong seven-year career with the AquaSox, fortified by the general manager to whom she reported. He was a big believer in giving his team exposure to the larger organization and baseball world, an expert at putting Katie into new positions where she could be successful.

Let us be real for a moment. Joyce was a trailblazer in an athletic world that was male dominated; Katie Woods was also knocking down doors for women in baseball. She shared with me that even six years into her professional career, she was fearful of how she might be treated once she shared the news of her pregnancy. Would her job be at risk? That same mentor she credits for supporting her eradicated archaic policies that were ignorant of women's needs and rights, initiating the efforts to create a maternity leave policy to protect Katie and those women who would come after her.

Katie's talents catapulted her into larger leadership roles. She proudly shared with me that she was named the Northwest League's Woman Executive of the Year for the first time in 2013, followed up with her being named again in 2015. Katie reminisced about how she was well established through her tenure with the AquaSox. In her assistant general manager role, she "yet still didn't know what the position meant to her" when it came to being a mother in baseball. Policies were not in place, nor were doors opening for qualified women who wanted to make it in the business of baseball. Katie shared that those inequalities resulted in the loss "of talented women right out of the gate."

Katie is proud that she and other successful women in baseball are setting new precedents that people can see, spurring newfound beliefs that dreams can come true for the next generation of talented young women.

Woods went on to talk about barrier breakers and the need for more traction for women in sports. Hap Dumont, founder of the NBC, had a woman, Lorraine Heinisch, umpire in two games in the 1943 tournament. This major step eight decades ago has not been recognized or repeated by Major League Baseball to this day.

Katie went on to win a third award, the 2019 Woman of Excellence, while with the Lancaster JetHawks. At that time, the team was affiliated with the

Colorado Rockies, playing in the California League. Unfortunately, as with many aspects of life changed by the COVID-19 pandemic, this team is no longer in existence.

Katie and her family now happily live in Wichita, Kansas. There was always a Kansas connection—her father was born in Kansas while her grandfather served at Fort Riley. The gateway to Wichita opened for Katie when she took on a leadership role with the Wichita Wind Surge, the AA affiliate for the Minnesota Twins. The fit wasn't great for her, as she felt that she had more to offer an organization in a potential general manager role.

Katie Woods and the National Baseball Congress crossed paths shortly thereafter. They accidentally found each other in the transition time, when Katie was interviewing for potential general manager roles in Minor League Baseball. She offered to help work at the 2022 National Baseball Congress World Series Tournament. The rest is history.

Katie, enthusiastic about the game of baseball and driven to find community connections between organizations and their neighbors, saw glimpses of what made the National Baseball Congress, now ninety years old, special. Katie shared that for those attending the tournament, "It is so generational; it is so special. I could see all these little moments, there was a community feel there where everyone knew each other, fans coming to each year's tournament now with their kids and grandchildren."

Courage and the power of *teamwork* shine through when one spends time with Katie. The NBC, infused with new energy and focus after the Rich family took over the reins, became a nonprofit in 2014, formed by the City of Wichita, which clearly understood the importance of the NBC and its

NBC World Series logo. *Courtesy of NBC and Katie Woods.*

legacy and the positive impact emerging in Wichita and communities beyond the city limits.

Katie went to the search group that was looking for new leadership while engaged in helping the team on the ground with the 2022 tournament. Katie said to me, "I think this is my job," as if serendipity was in play. She told the team looking for a new director that when it came to the potential of the NBC, "I see it; let me go and do it."

As you know from reading the story about baseball's Barnum, Hap Dumont, the NBC was built on a foundation fueled by innovation and courage. Katie saw an opportunity for change, hearing one too many times people talk about what the NBC used to be. Hap's legacy had laid dormant for a while. Katie came into her new

Katie Woods, tournament director, NBC World Series. *Courtesy of NBC and Katie Woods.*

role, as the first woman director of the National Baseball Congress World Series Tournament in its ninety-year history, asking herself, "What is this thing? What makes it special and unique?"

"There is so much baseball over such a short period of time, thirty-five games in ten days," Katie said. "People plan summer vacations around the NBC Tournament."

Trailblazers, especially the women highlighted in this chapter, have consistently encountered skepticism about their abilities and their legitimacy in the roles they have earned. I asked Katie about this. "I understand that it's new and different for a lot of folks. People are trying to figure out what it looks like [with the first woman in the role of NBC Tournament director]. Sixteen managers will experience it for the first time [in 2024] and will be open to next time a female director is running an event."

She shared, "I think it is worth noting, it fits into what Hap was trying to do from the start. There has always been a spirit of innovation, a spirit of pushing boundaries." I asked her about the future goals for the NBC under her leadership and was struck by the power and exciting potential evolution in her answer: "The fabric of baseball has been lying dormant. There is much there to build upon. I want the National Baseball Congress Foundation to be a resource for the college summer leagues; I want the new digital history archives available to connect families to their memories of family who played."

Innovation is at the forefront of the outstanding news in September that the NBC Baseball Foundation will begin operating independently in 2025. Katie shared the following as the announcement was unveiled.

This independence gives us new opportunities to connect communities through baseball, from history and alumni to youth programming and of course elevating top amateur prospects through the NBC World Series.

Baseball is a game of community, history and connection. The National Baseball Congress has served as a stellar example of this for ninety years. Case in point is what Katie shared when highlighting the fortuitousness entangled in the air as she simply stated to the search team that this job was waiting for her to arrive.

She knew that she had an uncle who had managed a team from her home state, Washington, the Bellingham Bells, in the NBC World Series in Wichita in 1999. In her first year on the job, she learned that the original manager of the Bellingham Bells, Joe Martin, had brought his team to Wichita more than a dozen times between 1940 and 1964. She grew up playing softball at Joe Martin Field in Bellingham, not knowing that the tournament in which he built his team would one day be the tournament she led.

Woods's trailblazing story is inspiring, as she sets an example for those young women who want to have a role in baseball. It can be done, it is possible, thanks to pioneers such as Katie Woods.

Heads up, Joyce Barnes, a Kenosha Comet in 1943, hurled a baseball to Alex Hugo, a second baseman, baseball star and roving instructor for the Oakland Athletics, in 2024. What did you say? You want me to go on? Yes, this is a story worth sharing and celebrating!

"Tell me about your first softball game as a kid."

"My first softball game, I'm so excited but also nervous. I got ready, and my dad and I pulled up to the field, only to see all my teammates and their parents walking to their cars because the game was over. We had gotten a non-updated schedule, so I missed my first ever softball game."

Alex Hugo, back in her early days, was shy despite her athletic talents, and regardless of what game she was playing, she took it seriously. I can only imagine what the car ride home was like that day or how amped up young Alex was for her next game.

Hugo, born in Olathe, has accumulated awards, trophies and medals in softball and baseball, while simultaneously creating a wonderful life off the ball field. As a high schooler, Alex played basketball, softball and track/cross country. Early indications of the level of athlete she was growing into, both physically and mentally, were evident as our conversation continued to unfold.

> *I played as many sports as possible. The mental capacity you have to possess to excel at cross country was the best mental training I had, because you always want to quit. You have to hold yourself to a higher standard to do the things that you don't want to. Cross country—oh my God, it would be so embarrassing if I quit a race. I would find somebody ahead of me, I would keep up with them, sit on their shoulder. I knew I was a better sprinter; in the end, I would try to have a good kick. It was kind of like a rush. If you go long enough, put in the time and work, there will be something beneficial waiting for you.*

Alex's drive and power of positive thinking proffered itself on the softball field in 2012, when she was playing for Olathe South, as she was selected as the Sunflower League Player of the Year.

In her formative years, Alex never idolized any ballplayers. Her mindset, no doubt shaped by her love-hate relationship with cross country, was that, if given the opportunity, she could always be better than those with whom she was competing. The confidence in her abilities started separating her from most of her competition. She loved watching the Royals, in awe of their athleticism. Alex shared with me, "Baseball is a romantic game, it is different, it is fun."

We will get back to baseball in a moment. Alex arrived at the University of Kansas, ready for her freshman year. A star in high school, eighteen years old, she quickly excelled on the softball diamond, hitting fifteen home runs and putting up exceptional stats. She confessed that her time at the University of Kansas was unsettled, despite early athletic success: "I was not in a good head space."

She wanted the opportunity to play on a bigger stage, perhaps in the SEC, with the goal of playing in a College Softball World Series. Everything fell into place on her first day as a Georgia Bulldog, when she slipped on her red, black and white softball uniform. Alex had a large chip on her shoulder when she transferred. She had always dreamed of playing in the SEC, with the opportunity to play against Alabama and other teams she had watched on ESPN. She had dedicated that summer at home prior to her first year as a Bulldog to getting stronger and improving her skills. She said, "My sophomore year was my best year; it was redemption. It helped ease me into the level of competition I played the next three years."

Alex Hugo, Georgia Bulldogs All-American second baseman. *Courtesy of Alex Hugo.*

Picture this athletic second basemen getting into a game-ready mindset, her teammate Taylor Schlopy, who was their centerfielder, nearby. One aspect of her rituals was her eye black prep. Alex was not the most popular kid growing up, as she chose to do things her own way, not caring what others thought. She wanted to be different on the field. She did not want to go the traditional route, with eye black straight across under both eyes, resting high on her cheekbones. When I first watched a video of her playing, I was struck by Alex, ball cap low, intense eyes focused on the next play, with straight eye black enhanced by vertical lines of eye black dropping off both ends of the straight line, creating an aggressive mark, reminiscent of a pi symbol. "I like it because it makes me look a little tougher, so maybe I will feel a little more confident that day."

Alex, in her first year suiting up as a Bulldog, became a standout star, knocking twenty-five balls out of the park. A kid who leveraged the eye black as a confidence booster, she went on to hit seventy-one home runs in her Georgia career, and she was recognized in her junior year as a second-team All-American. I watched some game action from her days in Athens. I recall seeing images of this super athletic defensive second basemen catching a soft fly in shallow right centerfield, spinning like an Olympic skater and, off one foot, doubling the runner off at first; Alex racing to catch another fly ball in shallow left center; and Alex gloving a Texas Leaguer, with Taylor, Georgia's center fielder and Alex's future wife, sliding at her feet to avoid colliding with her.

You may wonder why the three images I recalled were all of defensive plays.

> *Defense is my personal passion. I love the infield because it is an incredible space to let your leadership come out. It is so quick, so contagious for things to go wrong. It is always something different, a random hop, a different read on every pitch....It is very free to me.*

Alex loved defense, the collaboration and *teamwork* that was required to make plays. A favorite defensive memory she has comes from a game against Florida in the Super Regionals on a ball hit toward first base. "I was reading the ball and playing on it, even though it was clearly in the first baseman's path. She ended up missing it; I dove and got it, flipped it to her. She did a great job of recovering and getting to the bag. It was like controlled chaos in a way!"

The stats I have shared about Alex's hitting prowess from her first days on the diamond to games at Jack Turner Stadium in Athens cannot be ignored. While watching videos of her, I also witnessed Alex's aggressive open stance and fiery eyes staring down the pitcher as she wiggled her bat, waiting for the next pitch. Whether she drove the ball over the left centerfield fence or dragged a bunt down the third base line to cross home or first safely, her intensity exploded through her fist pump.

I asked Alex to share several of her fondest memories from her Bulldog days: "Sophomore year, in the regionals, we played the toughest game I can remember, fighting through fourteen innings, losing by one. It was a true test of mental toughness and banding together as a team, win or lose."

She and her teammates came back that night to play North Carolina. In the bottom of the seventh, the team fought back to tie the game. Guts and courage were on exhibit moments later, when Alex's high-spirited teammates welcomed her at home plate after her walk off home run, jumping up and down and enveloping her into the Bulldogs mob. What has continued to make Alex great is her combination of intensity, passion for the game and dedication to her team that started in her high school days, flourished through her Bulldog journey and culminated in her approach with Team USA.

The memories of that home run stayed with Alex in her first days as an Akron Racer in the now-defunct National Pro Fastpitch Softball League.[43] She was selected tenth in the draft and joined the Racers for a shorter-than-anticipated professional career.

Alex found herself at an inflection point athletically and in life. One of Alex's teammates at Akron suggested that she should consider trying out for the USA Women's Baseball team.[44] Trust me, Alex was skeptical. She had never played baseball, which she knew to be a much different game through her years of watching her hometown Royals play.

"Do I belong here?"

In writing this book, it struck me how often great ballplayers questioned their ability to play at the highest level.

"Now, I feel like I have stepped onto another planet."

Alex showed up and looked out at over one hundred female baseball

Alex Hugo, second baseman, USA Women's National Baseball team. *Courtesy of Alex Hugo.*

players, taking ground balls and hitting on a field with much different dimensions than those she was used to. What transpired? Alex made it through the mind-over-matter struggle, tackling fears of adjusting to a different game. The distance between the bags was greater. Her swing mechanics needed to change, and she needed to make new defensive adjustments. She told me that some of the people she is now closest to are the same women who clung together for support as they figured the game out day after day. "I opened a different life. Baseball is so diverse, it is so dynamic, and there is always a place for you if you want to stay in the game."

Alex has continued to develop her skills in the game of baseball—and in life. As I teased earlier, Alex and her teammate

Taylor were married on April 20, 2018. That same year, the USA Women's Baseball team (without Alex) came up short, in fact, not medaling in the Women's Baseball World Cup.

Alex's debut on the international stage came in 2019; she hit the ball field running and hasn't stopped since. What did she do? She batted .652, hit four home runs, drove in eighteen runs, helped the team win gold and went on to be named the tournament MVP, later in the year winning the USA Baseball Sportswoman of the Year Award. Then the COVID-19 pandemic hit. Alex and Taylor's first child, Finn, was born in 2020. Balancing life since then has become challenging for the couple. This was highlighted in 2024, as Finn turned four and Alex made a run at another gold medal with Team USA.

None of what has transpired in Alex's adult life would be possible without her wife, Taylor, who, according to Alex, is the "glue to this family." "We are thankful; we wanted to be on this path. Taylor has been so gracious blessing us with two sons." Alex and Taylor welcomed Fisher to their family on September 20. The challenges that Alex must overcome to maintain her level of skills have become more challenging as the home life she leads with her partner becomes richer. No matter how busy she becomes, one thing Alex counts on is Taylor's dedication to making "sure that we are all going to participate" in life at home, with their children, dogs and chickens.

Alex has gone on to not only play second base and take on a leadership role with the USA Women's team but also join and thrive in Home Run Derby X, which returned to four Major League parks in 2024.[45] Alex is one of five women who play in this twist on the classic Home Run Derby, which I used to study on our black and white television. They play three-on-three, with each team consisting of a retired major leaguer, a woman starring in baseball or softball and a yet-to-be-named local ballplayer from the city they are traveling to. The competition centers on each batter getting two and a half minutes to hit as many homers as they can. The catch is that the opposing team can take points away by making catches and robbing home runs from the bats of all, including Alex. The nonstop action ends after thirty minutes of play. Fans in 2024 enjoyed watching Jake Arrieta, Andruw Jones, Nick Swisher, Dexter Fowler, USA Women's National teammate Ashton Landell and, of course, Alex.

Taylor supports Alex with her different commitments, including hitting instruction for others, her Derby X travel, the 2024 Women's Baseball Classic, as well as, get this, her new role as a roving instructor for the Oakland Athletics.

Alex Hugo, Oakland Athletics roving instructor. *Courtesy of Alex Hugo.*

Alex loves her opportunities to mentor young girls and women, who have their own aspirations. "My biggest focus and message is 'don't be afraid to say yes.'" She reminds them (as she has reminded herself for years) that if it makes you uncomfortable, it could be a good thing. Pushing yourself out of your comfort zone to try something new can create opportunities. I shared with Alex a personal anecdote that I gravitated toward as a teenager, due to the instability of my high school years, as I found myself in a new state and a new school. In my later adult life, I got my mantra, courage over comfort, tattooed on my left forearm as a daily reminder.

An opportunity emerged for Alex to take on a coaching role with the A's. She thoughtfully reflected on this time, telling me, "If I had stayed in my comfort zone, I would have said no to the opportunity."

Her biggest anxiety was what the interaction with the guys would be like. Was she going to be able to relate to them? Will they take her seriously? Alex has succeeded and, in fact, thrived in this new role. She shared, "Regardless of what you think they know or what they think they know about you, if you are confident in what you are saying, if you believe in what you are saying, they will genuinely trust you."

In her roving instructor role, Alex has done everything from pitching batting practice to helping with swing mechanics, all with the intent that she can do something to help with players' development. It was no surprise to me when Alex said, "I am partial to infield instruction. I love defense."

Alex enlightened me on the great atmosphere her parents let her establish when she was a kid, forming the skills in Olathe that she now displays on an international stage. In her life, Alex never feared a car ride after a game. She was typically upset at herself for any miscues. Her parents did not create a negative climate for her and instead always starting the post-game drive home with, "What do you want to eat?"

She hopes to help influence this positive outlook for kids and their parents at every opportunity. She has met too many kids who are scared to get in their cars, and she has seen the negativity over something so simple and beautiful, the game they played that day, ruin important family dynamics.

So, what is next for this north star barrier breaker who came from Olathe? Alex starred in the 2023 Group A qualifying tournament to get to the WBC. She was named the Most Outstanding Player, with Ruth-like stats, batting .714 and going 10–14 over the four games, with 5 extra base hits and a crazy on base average of .773.

Alex and her teammates pushed Japan hard, winning a game versus them before losing in the championship game. Winning silver is a source of inspiration to young girls across the globe.

"THIS IS GOING TO BE SOMETHING THAT NOBODY IS GOING TO BELIEVE"

Gene Stephenson, retired coach of
the Wichita State University baseball team.

DETERMINATION
Staying focused on a plan, even though the path to its end may be different.

I wondered what my first meeting with Coach Stephenson, no. 10, was going to be like as I stepped out of my car in front of his home. I had read quite a bit about Coach, immersing myself in *Wichita Eagle* newspaper archives and turning every page of a book titled *Wichita State Baseball Comes Back*, by John E. Brown.

I had prepared a list of questions for this meeting. I pictured myself as an artist with a blank canvas under my arm, paintbrush in my hand and small paint cans of black and Shocker yellow (it has its own Pantone color, PMS 116C) stowed in my backpack.[46] Artistically, my goal was to take the blank canvas and capture the magic of our time together through every brush stroke and drop of Shocker yellow.

The drive through the Flint Hills, under a lazy summer sky, with hills and valleys rolling off in the distance like mellow ocean waves, had given me time to reflect. I was doing justice to the stories, connecting them through their Kansas fingerprints, as well as through honoring Jackie Robinson and League 42 by linking each chapter to one of the nine values.

I had set the table for this chapter, understanding that *determination* was the value that I so clearly witnessed through my research of Coach Stephenson.

What I did not realize was how the next 150 minutes of conversation with Coach would influence my approach to his story.

I was greeted at the door by Coach, who was sporting a Shocker polo shirt, wearing sneakers in Shocker yellow, smiling and asking me, "Are you there?" Gene's eyes still carried that intensity in them, the muscle memory still strong after thirty-six years of leading the Shocker program to greatness.

After meeting Gene; his wife, Jana Howser-Stephenson; and Shoxie, their wonderful five-year-old "puppy," in the entryway, I was graciously sent downstairs by Jana to relax and talk with Gene.

I stepped into a large space that was beautifully decorated, with sunshine warming the room and welcoming us. I was overwhelmed as I looked everywhere, my eyes dancing across the walls, registering history, life, triumph and greatness that was all beckoning me to come closer, listen, look and digest what a thirty-one-year-old newly hired coach of a dead baseball program built.

"THERE WAS NOTHING HERE."

Who is Gene Stephenson? He is a proud man, full of emotions, a potpourri of happiness, satisfaction, love, brotherhood, trauma, sadness, grief and a childlike amazement. I witnessed these emotions and more while surrounded by the gallery that Coach brought to life through our conversation and walking tour.

Who is Coach? He is an Oklahoma kid who, through his life journey, has carried, embraced, believed and instilled in the young men he led all nine of Jackie Robinson's life values.

How did he do it? I will tell you by forging ahead in this chapter, sharing stories of the Shocker program that Coach built while connecting each of them to one of the nine values: *persistence, courage, excellence, citizenship, justice, determination, commitment, integrity* and *teamwork*.

INTEGRITY
Sticking to your values regardless of what you think you should do.

Gene grew up in Guthrie, Oklahoma. Life did not come easy for the Stephenson family. Gene's dad quit school in the sixth grade. His mom quit school after her sophomore year of high school. His parents knew demanding work and were both full of Oklahoma grit. Gene's dad was quick to reinforce the importance of right and wrong through his own actions. He learned that there was no middle ground, no safe place, no gray. Actions were either right or wrong. Gene's dad taught him that a word given to someone, solidified through a strong handshake, represented commitment that would stand the test of time.

Gene learned the importance of *integrity* through his dad's teaching, remembering one's word could never be broken. Coach faced life challenges that fundamentally tested and redefined every core value he held.

Coach Stephenson exuded a hardscrabble toughness as he stepped onto the marching band practice field with his inaugural team for the first time. "I just never entertained the thought that we would fail," he said. He emphasized positivity with his players, holding each of them to his exacting standards of work ethic. He knew as he built the team, securing commitments from parents and their young sons, that his pledge was that education would come first—but baseball was a close second. Through the first few years as a coach, the team came together, fighting off opponents as well as the challenges of practicing on Little League ball fields and in empty gymnasiums across the city. The Shockers won just under 75 percent of their games in their first four years under Coach, setting the stage for 1982.

The Wichita State baseball program had a momentous year in 1982. Coach shared that the run to the national championship game against Miami would more than likely not have happened without God stepping in during the offseason. Seven starters were drafted off his 1981 squad. The team, led by Joe Carter in his final year as a Shocker, did not perform to the level of excellence that Coach demanded. Stephenson was frustrated as the season closed, as he realized that every bold statement he made at his introductory press conference back in 1977 had been met and exceeded by his boys. Yet, he had no bleachers and no dugouts despite raising money for the athletic department. Had he made a mistake? He had promised that his vision off the field would come true as well. Where was it?

These frustrations influenced four of his guys to not sign professional contracts as juniors during the offseason. This is where God might have stepped in, triggering a commitment to support Coach and his Shockers on their journey to greatness.

Phil Stephenson broke his jaw while playing in the National Baseball Congress World Series at the close of the Shocker season. He had been drafted by the Montreal Expos, who kept the offer on the table after his injury but did not budge financially. Phil decided to stay and play his senior year. His return to the Shockers was momentous, considering the NCAA Division 1 record forty-seven-game hitting streak he put together in 1981. Gene's younger brother of fifteen years was on his way to setting Division 1 career records by the time the 1982 season ended, including runs, hits, stolen bases, walks and total bases.

Charlie O'Brien, the starting catcher for Coach and the general behind the plate, committed to stay. Born in Tulsa, Oklahoma, O'Brien was determined by the age of five to be a catcher as good as Johnny Bench, and he delivered in 1982. As a senior, he established two WSU records, hitting 25 home runs and driving in 116 runs.

Don Heinkel, one of the best pitchers on the team, was determined to graduate and become a doctor. It was an easy decision for Don to make. He became the third piece of the puzzle and had a record of 16–5 as a senior in 1982, when he helped lead the Shockers to their first-ever appearance in the College World Series. Heinkel wrapped up his career by setting school records for games started, complete games, innings pitched and earned run average.

The puzzle was completed when Jim Thomas, an infielder extraordinaire and a speedster, opted not to sign with Houston, who drafted him in the eighth round. He came back and delivered, leading the country in hits and triples (in his final year). Thomas ended his Shocker career with a .351 average.

Coach told me that without those four guys and their leadership, "we weren't anything." The big four led by example, day in and day out, and were a threat to dominate whether they were in the field, at bat or on the mound. This 1982 team fit together well.

Integrity came into play early in the season when Coach took his team to square off with Arizona State. His boys played well, despite their limitations in practice in the winter climes of Wichita, losing the first two games, each by one run. The closing game was a disaster. The Shockers suffered their worst loss ever under Coach Stephenson, getting shellacked 18–0. What made matters worse was the poor gamesmanship exhibited by ASU. In the bottom of the eighth, the home team decided that it was OK to steal a base. The Sun Devil ballplayers were also relentless, trash talking, disparaging the stunned Shockers and using the phrase "Bananaramas" to make fun of their loud, yellow uniforms.

Coach Stephenson knew that ASU would be coming to Wichita near the end of the season. The lack of integrity shown by the victors stuck in the guts of the Shockers. Coach and the team had been close to stirring it up on the field with the Sun Devils but knew that was not the right thing to do. Instead, they would deliver their payback through a series victory in early May.

COURAGE
Doing what you know is the right thing, even when it is hard to do.

Gene had always dreamed of playing football for the University of Oklahoma. Uncertainty sat like a storm cloud over Norman when he was recruited. Longtime coach Bud Wilkinson announced that he was retiring. Coach Eddie Crowder moved on to Colorado, leaving the Sooners in disarray. The Arkansas program, led by a young football coach named Barry Switzer, had interest in recruiting Gene. The two hit it off, but Gene did not like their baseball program. Meanwhile, Coach Dan Devine of Missouri visited their home three times in the spring of 1965. Dreams of being a Sooner were put away; Gene was heading to Mizzou.

In his first year at Missouri, Coach Devine led the team to a Sugar Bowl victory, 20–18, over the Florida Gators. Gene's days of playing football ended due to a significant neck injury.

Stephenson's grit and talents served him well as the captain of the baseball team in 1967, his senior year. After graduating, with his wife of two years by his side, Gene did two things: he stepped up to serve and was commissioned into the army, and he took a graduate assistant position for the Missouri baseball team in 1968 before heading overseas.

Courage enveloped Gene's almost three years of military service. During basic training, Gene and his wife jumped at the opportunity to move to Berlin for active duty. Gene had the opportunity to continue working on his coaching skills after he accepted a request from a general's office to be the division baseball coach. By the time Gene turned twenty-three, he and his wife were parents, welcoming their son into their military household in Berlin. The three-year commitment Gene gave was attractive; he was told he would not have to get his boots muddy in Vietnam.

This Oklahoma kid, a young man in uniform, found the experience intriguing and frightening at the same time. He was two hundred miles inside East Germany. Everywhere he looked, the wall stood, dark and foreboding. "It was a terrible thing to watch and be part of." Tension existed whenever he had to travel. Trouble with the East Germans was one bad move, one misstep away.

Gene was sent to Vietnam despite promises made by the army. This was the first point in our time together when Gene showed raw emotions. His eight months in Vietnam, moving between Chu Lai, Da Nang and Long Binh Post, all U.S. bases, were brutal, painful and haunting.

> *The things that you see, you know, are different. There was a time where I was so miserable that I didn't think I was going to make it. I decided to write letters to coaches that I knew from colleges that I had played against, including my own coach, asking for a job. I was begging for someone to write me back, to give me some hope.*

His desperation to get home was answered by just one coach. He had met Enos Semore back in 1967, the year that Semore won the Junior College World Series with his Bacone College team.[47] Winning that championship in Muskogee, Oklahoma, launched Semore on to Norman, where he took over the Oklahoma program. Coach Semore (to this day, the winningest baseball coach in Oklahoma University history, with 851 wins) wrote to Gene, saying, "I have a graduate assistant job. It will be available if you get back."

The young officer exemplified *courage*. He had made sense of the madness he was living in during the war. He had taken the leap of faith, reaching out to coaching contacts asking for work, all while living on the Long Binh Post (which was attacked twice during the Tet Offensive), with incoming fire a nightly routine.

First Lieutenant Stephenson was given a choice months after landing in Vietnam. He could be promoted to captain and stay for the full year or remain a first lieutenant and get a four-month early out. "It took me about five seconds to let them know."

TEAMWORK
Working with other people toward a common goal.

The Stephenson family came back to Norman. Gene, then twenty-three years old, had a $2,000 baseball job and a GI Bill that would set him up to get his graduate degree. *Teamwork* unfolded immediately between Coach Semore and Graduate Assistant Stephenson. After Stephenson peppered his coach with questions about scholarship usage and comments about what the Oklahoma roster needed to compete nationally, Semore put him on the road.

He was out recruiting almost every day, looking to double the size of Oklahoma's pitching staff and offer the last nine full scholarships they had to build the team.

What transpired at OU? Over the five years that Stephenson was there, the Sooners made it to the World Series each year. Gene also became the first ever full-time assistant coach in the Big Eight Conference. Semore and the Sooners achieved quick success thanks to Gene's recruiting talents and dogged determination.

Getting back to our time together in Gene's Shockers gallery, teamwork rang true as a central piece of the belief system that Coach put in place with the program: "It was always about we, us and ours. Never about I, me and my."

I asked Coach a question, connecting the movie *Rudy* to his program, as I wanted to hear about his Rudy-like players. "We had a lot of them. We had certain things that we believed. You gotta believe in your team and help your teammates. You have to be a team guy to overcome difficulties."

Teamwork was exhibited across two playing fields at WSU. Phil Fulmer, offensive line/linebacker coach at Wichita State, was heavily recruiting Joe Carter to play football. Joe told Coach Fullmer that he wanted to come to WSU to play baseball for Coach Stephenson, who had been recruiting Carter in his days at OU. Fullmer had full rides in his arsenal; Stephenson hardly had anything to offer. Phil said, "Well, I can't get him to sign with us. Tell you what, we will give him a full, and you can tell his family that. At the end of his freshman year, if he doesn't want to play football anymore, we will keep him on the full football scholarship until his last day as a Shocker."

Coach hit the back of the leather couch when he finished this story. He was excited, fueled by the memories of the teamwork among coaches and the determination they had to land Joe Carter at WSU.

EXCELLENCE
Doing the best that you can.

Did Coach Stephenson and the Shocker program ride a wave of *excellence* for thirty-six years? They sure did. Under Stephenson's watch, the Shockers didn't have a losing season. The scrappy coach managed the Shockers to 26

Missouri Valley Conference season championships, winning the year-end title 18 times. His teams made 7 College World Series, winning the one in 1989. They made 26 NCAA tournaments, putting 1,837 wins in the record books. Coach shared his recruiting philosophy with me: "You try to recruit guys who are not only good athletes but can really run. I wanted to be a team that scared the living shit out of you. Every time we went to play, if you couldn't throw us out, we are going to run you out of the ballpark. If you get that reputation, your guys love to play like that. Teams that you are playing, they get a little scared and shaky."

After the Shockers swept a doubleheader late in the 1982 season against Arizona State, stealing six bases that Sunday, ASU Coach Brock said, "We didn't handle their running game well. Our biggest inability was stopping them from stealing any base they wanted anytime they wanted to."[48]

The Shockers knew one speed under Stephenson's leadership. They played as a team, feeding off each other's energy, determined to do the best they could.

DETERMINATION
Staying focused on a plan, even though the path to its end may be different.

Joe Carter, Wichita State University right fielder, succeeded, through endless effort, a never-ending *determination* to become better at the game of baseball.

Gene said, "I had been looking at Joe Carter since he was fourteen years old. He was an athlete. He did not know the first thing about how to play baseball. He was playing shortstop on an awful high school team. I knew we could develop him. The day that I announced that I was leaving OU for Wichita State, I told Big Joe and the family that I was going to keep trying to recruit Joe to come to WSU. We do not have anything yet, but I want to coach him." The response from Big Joe was music to Coach Stephenson's ears: "Well, let me tell you coach, wherever you are next year, that is where Joe is going to be."

Gene continued, "He had a lot of tools. I am going to make this guy turn into a player soon. He comes in and makes freshman All-American. He worked diligently on the things that he didn't do well. He would come out on his own to work on them. Out of nowhere, a guy who did not make any Oklahoma high school All-Star teams, wasn't drafted...one year later, every scout in America is talking about him possibly being the no. 1 pick after his junior year."

Carter became Wichita State's first ever All-American. In fact, he was selected as All-American for all three years as a Shocker. Carter achieved college greatness as his junior year ended, becoming the 1981 NCAA Player of the Year while putting his name in the Shocker record books for the highest batting average (.430) and slugging percentage (.788).

COMMITMENT
Making a promise and following through on it.

Stephenson talked about his emphasis with his kids on the approach they should take when something goes wrong: "If you can't do anything about the bad thing that happened [like four strikeouts in a game], figure out how it happened and see how you are going to fix it." He went on to talk about how the typical human reaction when something goes wrong is to say, "Why me?" He demanded *commitment* from his kids—they had to be tougher-minded than that. Instead of his team saying they don't deserve a bad thing, he wanted them to fix the situation and believe they were doing the right thing. Coach loved ballplayers who were committed to the program, who loved and respected the game and who played with a fire in their belly. He challenged his ballplayers through the years to embrace what he called the *Five Ds*, which were: *Deserve It* (believe that you deserve success through hard work), *Desire* (the fire that burns), *Dream, Discipline* and *Dimension* (keep things in perspective, stay balanced). He continued, "What is important is the legacy that you leave. All those guys know I gave them my best. I know they gave their best. It is an unbreakable bond with them."

Stephenson was quoted at his February 1977 press conference, as saying, "I'm planning on a four-year program. In the fourth year, hopefully, we will be in a position to challenge for the college world series—hopefully sooner."[49] Coach believed in his vision, committing himself to achieving his yearly goals in front of a hungry Wichita press: "I don't know how many believed me, but I believed it."

Stephenson stepped onto the campus in the spring of 1977 as head coach of nothing. He had no field, no equipment, no players, no assistant coaches. What he did have was a drive to succeed and to do something that had never been done before.

We came from nothing, no seats, no field, no place to practice, no support. I am out there beating the bushes every day. Where are you going to play? We practice on the marching band practice field with no backstop. I always believed you could do something from nothing if you believed in what you were doing and could make believers of the people around you. You keep those people who believe the same dream.

His first team, the 1978 squad, won forty-three games! He stressed to his players that he wanted them to understand and believe in the work they were doing. He had a long-standing practice of telling his ballplayers, "We work on things that we don't do well that are things that are required to do well if you are going to win." Coach came alive and pointed his finger at me. Energized, coaching me up, he said, "Get your ass out on your own, and we will work together. It is going to make you better, our team better."

I know with the utmost certainty that Gene Stephenson is a visionary. It could have all started back in his godforsaken days in Vietnam, when he knew that a response from just *one* coach would give him hope and an opportunity to be what he wanted to be.

He took on this job, stating that, although there was nothing, he knew that this was going to be the first time anything like this had ever been done in baseball. He had a vision that also included what the stadium would look like. He had an architect bring his dream to life; the rendering is now proudly positioned on a wall that faces the sitting area in the middle of Gene's gallery. "That was my dream," Gene said, his voice full of emotion.

His innate ability to find athletes, though not necessarily ballplayers, for the program was legendary. Joe Carter was the highest mountain among a range of magnificent mountain peaks, young men who became ballplayers after seeing Coach Stephenson's vision, believing in it and working hard to get their college degrees and/or be drafted by Major League Baseball. His program helped 55 All-Americans blossom while playing at Eck Stadium. Over the thirty-six years Gene coached the Shockers, 159 players signed professional contracts, with 34 finally making it to the Major Leagues.

CITIZENSHIP
Making a contribution that improves the lives of others.

Gene and his wife, Jana, embody model citizenship. They both work tirelessly as members of the board of trustees of the College Baseball Hall of Fame. In addition, the WSU program received a planned gift in the amount of $600,000 from the Stephenson's in 2014. The gift, rightfully, had a restriction that it would be used only to support the baseball program, which I think is quite fitting.

Keep in mind that this gift was bestowed just over a year after the painful termination of Coach Stephenson's contract by Wichita State. I observed heartache and sorrow flowing from his eyes during our time together. Coach is a stubborn, driven, proud, resilient and committed man. The events that unfolded after the 2013 season were no doubt painful for the entire Shocker community. I could feel it as I navigated online reviews of the papers leading up to and including the sad day, when Coach walked away from the home he had built.

Had the program continued to win? Absolutely. Had they made the World Series in recent years? No. Had the program developed All-Americans and yearly draft picks? Not recently. Were doubters saying that Coach was past his prime, out of touch with what needed to be done to stay at the exceptional level that he had established? Yes.

The growing level of negative noise from the press and community had to be painful and hard to absorb for Coach Stephenson.

Pride in what he created, the lives he touched, his challenging work and the impossible becoming possible are what make his heart smile. I was witness to greatness that afternoon I spent with Gene.

Through his actions in 2014, Coach clearly wants the WSU Shocker baseball program to thrive for decades to come. Gene joked with me as our tour of the gallery was winding down, calling out that there was no more wall space for memorabilia: "That is why they fired me. We didn't have any more room!"

Gene shared a remarkable story about *citizenship* with me. That value rang true through the actions of Mrs. Gladys Wiedemann, a noted Wichita philanthropist. In May 1982, Wichita State and its baseball program received national exposure in a matchup with Arizona State, ranked no. 1 in the country, at Lawrence-Dumont Stadium, televised on ESPN.

Coach shared with the press that he still did not have any seats for fans at Eck Stadium. The Wichita sportswriters ignored the nationally televised game and all its potential favorable impact on the program, opting to talk about anything but the Shockers leading up to the game and the important series. Irascible Coach Stephenson blasted the local newspapers for their lack of coverage and support. Mrs. Wiedemann, leading the K.T. Wiedemann Foundation after her husband, Karl, passed, saw an opportunity to step up.[50]

By the next year, the first bleachers that Coach ever had were put in place on the Shockers' first base side. Of course, years have passed, and Eck Stadium has become magnificent among the national college ball parks. Tough, gritty Coach Stephenson has a sentimental side to him, which was illuminated when he made a point of not letting those bleachers be torn down. Instead, under his direction, they now stand proudly behind left field, embodying all that the "little engine that could" of Shocker baseball in the early days stood for.

Our time together was priceless. I believe that if one were to sit in that downstairs area on a quiet, late evening, they might hear the players chatting from their frames, reminiscing about their glory days, their winning days and seasons they were part of with the Shockers and Coach Stephenson.

I left one value, *justice*, to bring the story home for another Shocker win.

JUSTICE
Treating all people fairly, no matter who they are.

I had the opportunity to have breakfast with Gene's pitching coach, Brent Kemnitz, one morning. Justice is a value that is best illustrated in this baseball journey that Coach Semore, Coach Stephenson and Coach Kemnitz are all connected through.

Coach Semore held a position open for a first lieutenant who was serving in Vietnam so he could join him with the Oklahoma Sooner baseball program. Stephenson, who was twenty-three years old at the time, was given his first opportunity to make a name for himself. Coach Semore took a chance. What transpired over the next five years was a magical run to the NCAAs each year, fueled by tireless recruiting that Stephenson drove, putting miles under his wheels and bringing good ballplayers to the Sooner dugout. His readiness to take the next step was advanced through the ownership Semore gave Gene.

I like the symmetry this story takes as it closes, because the favor was paid forward again. Coach Stephenson invited a then twenty-one-year-old Brent to two meetings, with the hope that he could convince this Oklahoma kid to move into the Fairmount Towers on campus with the team, making pennies full of future promise. In their first meeting, Gene blew Brent away, saying, "This is how it is going to happen," as he detailed the four-year plan. Kemnitz, a college pitcher who knew he had hit his playing ceiling, was given the opportunity to come up to Wichita.

Coach Stephenson handed the pitchers over to his new pitching coach/graduate assistant. Brent shared that "he didn't know if I was any good, but he knew they would outscore teams!" Brent's secret to his success under Coach Stephenson was his approach with the staff, "speeding up their brains," building their confidence up while breaking down their shortfalls so they could absorb what they needed to do. Kemnitz bought into the vision Gene had, helping nineteen of his guys reach the Major League level.

Coach Stephenson also handed a list of professional scouts with details, four or five pages long, to his new graduate assistant. "These guys are going to help us; we need to build our program." Suddenly, a scenario was playing out in 1977 between a coach and his young graduate assistant that was eerily like what a twenty-three-year-old took ownership of years ago in Norman, Oklahoma, in one of his first meetings with Coach Semore. They both became exceptional recruiters, committing to families that their sons would get their educations and have opportunities to become successful whether on a ball field or in an office.

Coach Stephenson is worth celebrating. His actions over his thirty-six-year career bring Jackie's nine values into focus. He was the man responsible for creating a great program, the best that our Sunflower State has ever had. Thank you, Coach!

KANSAS BOYS, BIG-LEAGUE BALLPLAYERS

EXCELLENCE
Doing the best that you possibly can.

Mitch Webster

For what shall a man be profited,
if he shall gain the whole world, and forfeit his life?
—Matthew 16:26 [51]

"I watched the guys on TV. I loved Rose, Clemente and Mays. I tried to emulate those guys," Mitch Webster said to me as he recalled his early days playing the game. Mitch, born in Larned, Kansas, did not have a high school team he could call his own. Gifted with speed, Webster ran on the track team and played basketball and baseball, inspired by his dad who played professionally until his back told him no more. During his high school years, Mitch threw left-handed, batted right-handed and left puffs of dust in the wind as his cleats pounded the base paths into submission. At one point, his dad told him that there were not many guys in the big leagues who could throw and hit like his son could. Opportunities could be unlocked for Webster, assuming that he could adjust to the game and become a switch-hitter.

The year is 1977; the scene we cut to is one with Mitch, his dad and an area scout for the Dodgers in a conversation about his future in baseball in the family living room. On the table was a $10,000 contract with the opportunity to report to Lethbridge, Alberta, home of the Lethbridge Dodgers. The scout looked at the father and son and said he was going to leave the house and drive around the block several times to give them time to work things out. Mitch's dad looked at him and said, "This is your deal. You have always wanted to play big-league ball." Mitch laughed as he shared with me that it took him no more than two minutes to say yes, considering the limited scouting attention he had received.

Eleven games into his days as a Lethbridge Dodger, he had not left the bench. Once his coach, Gail Henley, penciled him into the lineup, Mitch did not look back. Coach Henley must have seen something special in Webster's game, because he found a way to look beyond the initial woes Mitch had when running to first base. Comically, Mitch kept missing the bag when running to first, thrown off by the intrusion of a long jump technique drilled into his memory called the hitch-kick. "In the long jump," Mitch said, "when you miss the board, you just run through." Coach pulled the young man into his office, looked at him in disbelief and asked, "What are you doing?!" Coach started yelling and said, "You can't stutter step and hit first base!" Fines of one dollar were thrown his way until Mitch overcame this fusion of the two sports.

Eleven years passed. Mitch experienced the pitfalls of being a draft pick of the Toronto Blue Jays in their inaugural season and the good fortunes of sharing the outfield turf with Tim Raines and Andre Dawson with the Expos, eventually landing with the Chicago Cubs in 1988. Let me expand on this journey. Mitch spent five years toiling in the Minors for Toronto, struggling to find an opportunity due to the young up-and-coming outfielders George Bell, Lloyd Moseby and Jesse Barfield. Traded to the Expos before the 1985 season, Mitch finally had his opportunity and, as he recollects, had his best years through 1987. The Expos were in the pennant race two of those three years, with Mitch playing a key role, batting .285 with 105 extra-base hits, averaging 35 steals a year.

I have Curt Nelson, senior director of the Royals Hall of Fame, to thank for piquing my interest in Mitch. He shared a story about Mitch becoming the first to have a hit in the historic first-ever Wrigley night game that vanished as the winds and rain pummeled Wrigley Field.

Picture Wrigley in all its glory on August 8, 1988 (8/8/88), with the Cubs' best pitcher, Rick Sutcliffe, taking the mound to start this historic game. In the bottom of the first, Mitch stepped to the plate and dug into the left-hand box, his shirt heavy with dampness from the humidity, and proceeded to drive a grounder past the diving Juan Samuel into centerfield on the first pitch he saw. As Webster checked the signs from the third base coach, Morganna Roberts, known as the Kissing Bandit, slipped over a low wall down the right field line and beelined it for the plate. Her goal was to kiss Ryne Sandberg on his cheek, adding another ballplayer to her growing list of successes dating back to her very first victim, Pete Rose, at Crosley Field in August 1969.

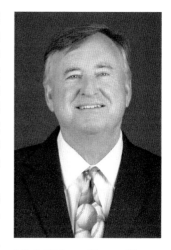

Bill Murray, comedian extraordinaire, was sharing the booth and possibly a pint or two with Harry Caray on this historic evening. Murray looked at Harry and quipped, "I couldn't see anything, Harry! I lost her in the lights!"[52] Sandberg composed himself after watching Morganna get escorted off the field,

Mitch Webster, Kansas City Royals scout. *Courtesy of the Kansas City Royals.*

her lipstick glistening, unmarked sans kiss. Ryno launched a two-run home run into the thick air to reclaim the lead for the Cubs, 2–1. That historic single by Webster is not recorded anywhere, washed from our memories as rain descended in sheets, giving Greg Maddux, Al Nipper and Jody Davis the opportunity to put on a "Casey at the Bat" pantomime on the tarp held down by deep puddles of Chicago rain. Mitch reflected about the game, "There was more fanfare than in playoff games. It was pretty cool, really."

As I wrapped up my interview with Mitch, I fired a couple of questions his way. His response to my question about the "toughest center field to cover," he answered that it was MacArthur Stadium in Syracuse, New York, where he played for the Syracuse Chiefs. Mitch described the field, which is no longer standing, "It was 434 feet to center with a 30-foot wall, gaps 410 feet. I didn't cover that outfield—I just tried." The next question thrown his way, "Who was the toughest pitcher you ever faced?" Mitch responded swiftly, eager to spit out what still left a bitter aftertaste in his mouth: "Nolan, 2 for 19, 12 punchouts. I was scared of him. Nolan threw it at my head because I tried to bunt off him in the first game I faced him. He had me. My last game, I tripled twice off Ryan."

I could not resist asking the next question, about what he did when standing on third after the first triple. Mitch shared, "I didn't look at him. I turned around and looked into the left field corner. I didn't want to see if he was mad, because I knew I had three more at-bats."

Webster's perspective about the game of baseball evolved through his career. The Bible passage at the start of this chapter serves as a reminder to Mitch that if a man inherits the whole world (which he thought he had as he became a major leaguer and starting centerfielder), it would not give him the peace and joy that he welcomes from knowing Jesus. Mitch, who has worked in the Royals scouting organization for fifteen years, spends his days on the road as a pro scout, sharing his baseball and spiritual wisdom with young ballplayers.

ALEX GEORGE JR.

I want to take us back to 1955, when a ball club packed up their gear, leaving Philadelphia for their new home, Kansas City. As this significant move was in the works, a young man was wrapping up his Rockhurst High School years, graduating with ten letters across three sports he excelled at, including basketball, football and, of course, baseball. The senior at Rockhurst had achieved a level of excellence across these sports due to his drive at an early age to do the best he could. This ultimately led him to have next-level ability. Alex George Jr. was looking forward to his University of Kansas future, knowing that he would continue to play basketball and baseball as a Jayhawk. While settling in on the hill at KU, he was introduced to another teammate, Wilt Chamberlain. On September 16, he received a call that reshaped his future. His dad told him that the new professional baseball team in Kansas City, the Athletics, had just offered him a contract.

Sixteen-year-old Alex drove home from Lawrence that evening. "It's all a strange circumstance," George shared, "everything was spur of the moment."[53] In front of his dad and A's Manager Lou Boudreau, George signed a contract for $10,000 for two years.

The minor-league seasons had been completed as September shook its leaves, thinking about gracing lawns with a blanket of color far into October. Alex arrived at Municipal Stadium, dressed to play the very next day, surrounded by ballplayers who quizzically wondered who the "new bat boy" was.

The sixth-youngest Major League player ever, Alex pinch-hit in his first game against the White Sox. He stepped up to the plate in the eighth inning, looking down at longtime catcher Sherm Lollar crouching behind the plate. George remembers, "I get into the batter's box, and I've got to tell you, my

Alex George,
1955 Kansas City
Athletics. *Courtesy of
the Kansas City Royals.*

knees are shaking so hard, maybe he felt sorry for me." Al Papai, a thirty-eight-year-old knuckleballer, looked in from the mound. Lollar, a Kansan, tried to calm the dancing sixteen-year-old Alex down. The conversation unfolded: "You ever hit a knuckleball?" "No." "You ever see a knuckleball?" "No." "That's all this guy throws. So, now you know what's coming."[54]

That at-bat concluded with a swing-and-miss strikeout for Alex, who headed to the dugout viewing the quick exit as a blessing. Who would have thought that his time on the big stage would last all of nine days? George appeared in five games, going 1 for 10. His one hit came from a successful drag bunt toward third against Tigers rookie pitcher Duke Maas. When the season ended, Alex packed up and returned to Lawrence to start his classes.

Although George's time in the big leagues falls far short of Mitch Webster's, Alex did go on to have a minor-league career, primarily with the Royals. He played eight years in the minors and hit eighty-one home runs before retiring from the game at twenty-four years of age. Alex played shortstop, bringing his speed and aggressiveness to the plate as a switch-hitting leadoff batter.

I ask that you pause for a moment after reading about Alex, who lives in Prairie Village. He was sixteen years old, signed by the Athletics and thrust onto the grand stage to play baseball on the same grass as teammates Enos Slaughter and Clete Boyer. Sixteen! To this day, Alex will occasionally receive mail with requests for his autograph. Memories in the game of baseball have been a way of connecting fans through the decades, finding common ground where wonderful stories can be shared. Let us honor Alex George Jr. by looking in awe at what this young man did on a diamond surrounded by grandstands on the corner of East Twenty-Second Street and Brooklyn Avenue, just months removed from his last game pitching on the high school field at Rockhurst.

LUTHER TAYLOR

It is a good thing Taylor can't tell stories,
or I never should be able to get any work out of you fellows.[55]
—John McGraw

One might wonder why I have gone back in time as I have shared these three ballplayers' stories. I have done this with intent, because you will be blown away by the story that I am about to share about Luther Taylor. Luther will take us back in time to the beginning of the twentieth century, when those who were not like everyone else were often shamed, ridiculed and called names. Let me not get ahead of myself though.

This Kansan was born in 1875 in Oskaloosa, home to just over seven hundred citizens at the time. As was typical in rural Kansas, Luther was born on a farm run by his dad, Arnold, and managed by his mom, Emaline. Taylor was not like the other kids. This youngster had dreams of someday becoming a boxer and visualized throwing a punch like Jack Dempsey. Taylor said, "But Ma and Pa objected." And he forever buried the thought of being in a ring.

Luther was born profoundly deaf. He attended the Kansas School for the Deaf in Olathe through his high school years, and there, his personality, courage, strength, perseverance and ability to play baseball matured like the wheat that blankets the rich Kansas soil on farms far and wide. Taylor ventured out from the shelter of his longtime school to play semiprofessional ball for a few years before his opportunity to step into the big leagues came about.

An underlying tragic element to this story is that society was not truly kind back in the day. "Dummy" became the crude "given name" for all deaf people. I will not refer to Luther as Dummy Taylor but just this once (unless it is framed in a quote from his days of playing ball), because I am intent on showing him the respect he deserves.

The scene is set, the date August 28, 1900. His team, the New York Giants, are to square off against the Boston Beaneaters. The opponents aggressively try to take advantage of the pitcher's deafness, attempting to steal third an amazing five times! In 1942, Taylor was quoted as saying, "I nailed each one. I walked over to Long, the last man caught, and let him know by signs I could hear him stealing."[56]

Luther quickly became a key piece of the Giants' rotation, starting forty-three games in his first full season, finishing an amazing thirty-seven of those starts. The Giants were punchless offensively, resulting in Taylor losing twenty-seven games. The next year was remarkable for Luther, as he took under his wing a rookie by the name of Christy Mathewson. That year, the Giants had not one deaf pitcher on the roster but three, never to be witnessed again in Major League Baseball.

The year 1903 was when the New York Giants, playing at the Polo Grounds, became a force to be reckoned with, as John McGraw stepped in as the Giants' manager. They quickly became one of the best teams in the National League, with Mathewson leading the way, followed by Taylor, who had his greatest season in 1904, winning twenty-one games. In 1905, the Giants won their second consecutive pennant. Luther came through again, winning sixteen games. Taylor had a tough time holding back his nerves and excitement on October 11, when he was scheduled to pitch the third game of the World Series. He realized that the deaf community would celebrate witnessing the first deaf major leaguer to ever pitch a World

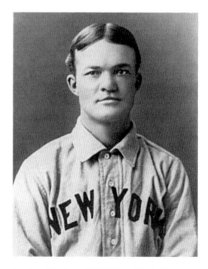

Luther Taylor, 1903 New York Giants. *Courtesy of Wikipedia.*

106

Series game. The weather didn't cooperate, however, washing away his opportunity and setting up Christy Mathewson to pitch again with the extra day of rest.

I have talked too much about his baseball career. I need to talk about Luther and his amazing resilience, his joyful approach to the game and his team and his demanding demeanor when it came to what he expected of Manager McGraw and his teammates.

Resilience is defined as "the ability to withstand difficulties and/or toughness." We can both agree that Luther had a trunk full of resilience that he carried every day of his life.

His joyful approach to the game was mentioned in the *New York Times* in April 1905: "The 'Dummy' [I was struck by this terminology being so pervasive, included in everything from conversations to print] is always smiling. No matter whether in the dressing room or on the practice field he is the clown of the crowd."[57]

The expectation that Luther set with McGraw, Mathewson and the rest of the team was that they would learn sign language so they could communicate with him. That they did; the power of persuasion is so high when one reflects on this demand. The irascible John McGraw was willing to learn sign language to make the team inclusive. Fred Snodgrass, a teammate of Taylor's, recalled in Lawrence Ritter's 1966 book, *The Glory of Their Times*,

> *We could all read and speak the deaf-and-dumb sign language, because Dummy Taylor took it as an affront if you didn't learn to converse with him. He wanted to be one of us, to be a full-fledged member of the team. If we went to the vaudeville show, he wanted to know what the joke was, and somebody had to tell him. So we all learned. We practiced all the time.*[58]

Fred's comments were best represented by watching Luther and his teammates on a typical train ride to the Polo Grounds to play another game. The Giants would practice sign language, including spelling out what advertising signs said. One of Jackie Robinson's nine values, *excellence*, comes to life in this story about Luther and his Giants teammates. The team, under the watchful eye of John McGraw, made winning pennants a habit, Luther developed into a top-tier pitcher and his teammates responded to his challenge to do the best they could to learn his "silent" language, bringing the Giants together in a deep, meaningful way.

Taylor was not only exceptional when on the mound (where he won 116 games in his career, with a 2.75 ERA), but he was also an entertainer on the other side of the foul lines. McGraw often had Luther coach first base on his off-days, and at times, he would express his displeasure with calls the umpire made. Comically, he would rotate his right hand by his head, pointer finger almost touching his temple, signaling for all to see that the umpire was not "all there." Luther's creative genius was remembered fondly by ballplayers—but not the umpires who were his targets.

Honus Wagner, a Hall of Famer, recalled a game played in conditions like those found in the Amazon rainforest, where the Giants were voicing their displeasure from their dugout, saying the game should be called. Bill Klem, the target of the day, watched as "Dummy Taylor, one of the Giant pitchers, went out to the third base coaching lines in his hip boots and raincoat. The umpire did get mad. He chased Taylor out of the park, and it was funny to see Dummy trying to explain to him that he shouldn't be ejected."[59] I was amazed when I read this story, laughing at the vision and believing that Luther's fatal faux pas was the lit lantern he held over his head!

My favorite story about Taylor is that of the day he received a bit of his own medicine when he was caught cursing Hall of Fame umpire Hank O'Day. O'Day, who grew up with one deaf parent, knew each curse word slung his way. He stepped in front of the plate and signed the following to Luther: "Listen, smart guy, I've spent all my spare time this past week learning your language. You can't call me a blind bat anymore. Now go take a shower. You're out of the game."[60]

Taylor was more than a ballplayer. He is credited by some with amplifying the use of sign language on baseball fields, including the use of pitching signs. When he retired, he focused on giving back, teaching and coaching at his former school, the Kansas State School for the Deaf as well as at the Iowa and Illinois Schools for the Deaf in the years ahead.[61] One of his proudest moments, which speaks to the man he was, occurred when Dick Sipek, a student and ballplayer Luther mentored, was signed by the Cincinnati Reds. He was the first deaf player to make it to the big leagues who was not characterized by the hostile nickname that Luther remembered with bitterness. Taylor was a gift to the deaf community and a believer in inclusivity for all, bursting with pride, aware that he was a pioneer on the national stage, living proof that the deaf should be integrated into society.

"BILL JAMES EATS AND BREATHES DIAMOND DUST"

Backstage with *Esquire*, April 24, 1979.

I am and have been since the age of eleven so utterly consumed by my interest in baseball that I have never been energetic enough to do anything else. I want to put out the most complete picture of the game that is available and never repeat anything that has been written before.
—*Bill James,* Esquire, *April 24, 1979*

PERSISTENCE
Working toward a goal and continuing to move forward,
even though you face obstacles or barriers.

Bill James, an army vet, showed up at his local university, Kansas University, intent on continuing to consume baseball statistics while working on his sideline gig, getting three degrees over a handful of years, in English, economics and education. There is no doubt that his childhood years influenced his multifaceted approach to his educational pursuits as a Jayhawk.

Personal tragedy befell Bill, first when he lost his mother to cancer at the age of five and then when his dad, years later, broke his back while trimming tree branches. Bill's childhood was fraught with challenges and instability, marked by a lack of the love and support we all need during our formative years.

Bill looked to sports, specifically baseball, as a safe place. The Kansas City Athletics captivated him, becoming his beloved home team. Despite season after season of losses, each spring, Bill looked to the Athletics as a team full of promise, though they were destined to fall short of his hopes and expectations. He loved to play sandlot ball during the long Kansas summers, but as with the Athletics, his ability to play the game did not improve.

Little did the world of baseball know that this kid, who immersed himself in baseball analytics during his childhood, would emerge on the national baseball map in the late 1970s. Bill, incredibly bright and curious, shifted the energy he had spent cheering on the hapless Athletics into learning about and understanding the analytical side of baseball. His obsession, obvious to those close to him, exasperated his sixth grade teacher, who, at one point, pulled the young boy aside and told him to quit wasting his time, exclaiming, "So what's all this crappola about baseball statistics?" However, his teachers saw an intellect emerging as well as an early leadership presence.

I learned through researching Bill's story that he has a mind of his own, a strong belief in his intellect, a disregard for naysayers (and especially editors) and an obsession to understand America's national pastime and share his knowledge with baseball nerds across the country, challenging all the traditional beliefs, customs and statistical records that the game was built on.

Bill's brain was in hyperactive mode from the moment the game wrapped him in its arms. As he realized that the Athletics would not become a top-tier team, he shifted his interest (from focusing on a team) to the game itself: "I… more or less misused my education to learn to analyze baseball."

I want to take us back to the early 1970s and Lawrence, Kansas. Bill came back from his military stint, enrolled at the University of Kansas and started his educational journey. Bill left a trail of diamond dust between the campus and his job as a Pinkerton night security guard at the former Stokeley Van Camp plant, pontificating about the game and devouring statistics. Saying he had an obsession is an understatement. Losing one's parents can leave a person untethered. I know this to be true, having lost my parents. I found myself empathizing and understanding Bill's inclination to bury himself in the game of baseball for nearly all his waking hours. The game and its statistics helped ground Bill; the writing and analysis that occupied his time while working and missing classes gave him solace and a spark.

Bill found opportunities to evaluate his theories through tabletop simulation baseball games that unfolded at a Lawrence restaurant fittingly named The

Ball Park. He dove deeper into the world of analytics, motivated, in this case, "to win that damn little league."

Bill used his first two degrees to further sharpen the skills that served as the foundation of his future endeavors. His economics degree opened his eyes to the application of mathematical modeling to determine if a hypothesis can indeed be true. His English degree continued to sharpen a talent he was born with, the ability to write prose that expressed his points of view with brutal clarity at times, coupled with a sharp sarcasm and love for the game that was always present.

Bill's tunnel vision left him susceptible to surprises. The biggest shock was his sudden dismissal from his security job, which had provided him hours of unchecked "work" time that he utilized to write and research.

His first book started to emerge in shape, format, content and texture.

Bill's first opportunity to share his thoughts on a national stage emerged in an article he wrote that was picked up by *Baseball Digest*, published as part of the November 1975 monthly edition. I have a copy of the issue, which I immediately felt connected to through the front cover image of Rookie of the Year Fred Lynn striding into a pitch in his home ballpark, Fenway.

His article, starting on page 41, titled "Winning Margins: A New Way to Rate Baseball Excellence," laid out Bill's approach to evaluating the sport's stars across the decades through a method of comparing winning margins in key statistics of greats versus the ballplayers who finished second. Those margins, he believed, could be used then to compare great performances across decades. He shared, "The value of these charts is that they help us to recognize brilliant performances that we might otherwise overlook when talking about all-time greats."[62]

The beauty of this innovative approach was to offer a baseball fan a unique perspective on how Rod Carew might stack up against Rogers Hornsby and Ted Williams in the statistical lane of batting averages—which the three ballplayers excelled at in their own careers.

Just over two years later, Bill bought a small, cheap column in *The Sporting News* to advertise his first annual *Baseball Abstract*. A small group of baseball nerds responded to the advertisement, sending a check or cash in the amount of $3.50 to Bill. In return, they received his self-published sixty-eight-page collection of reviews of eighteen categories of statistical information. He sold seventy-five copies of the first *Abstract*, which his wife had edited, put together, xeroxed, stapled and shipped to his first fans.

Did Bill make any money from his first ever *Abstract*? His production budget for the book, pulled together through his tireless efforts to tabulate box scores by hand, was $112.73. The gross sales generated from his tiny advertisement came to just over $260. He and his wife deposited around $100, a disparaging sum when considering the endless hours of work, advertising and shipping costs. Did the meager earnings stop Bill from coming back with a *1978 Baseball Abstract?*

The world of Sabermetrics came to life on the shoulders of Bill James, who tirelessly worked for the next eleven years to generate the yearly *Baseball Abstract*.[63] The crazy idea that there was a science of baseball statistics began to take shape through Bill's first self-publishing attempt. While Bill was working endlessly, straining his eyesight, pushing himself to exhaustion with the release of the next *Abstract*, I was living the life of a teenager in Exeter, New Hampshire, rolling dice in my Strat-O-Matic tabletop simulation game, tracking season statistics against records established in past years. In my opinion, I was a variant of Bill in his college days, oblivious to the transformation James was developing.

Bill called what he was doing "Sabermetrics," giving life to a new phenomenon that, over the following decades, would change the way fans and big-league organizations approached the game. Bill would take questions, issues and theories about the game and build his base of followers and early adopters by submitting the theories to tests and modeling. Bill's greatest talent was his ability to consolidate what he deemed worthy for each successive *Baseball Abstract* into statistical chapters that were powerfully brought to life through his writing talents.

Bill James

The fearless forecast of the '79 baseball season (on pages 64–67) comes exclusively to Esquire from Bill James, a twenty-nine-year-old fanatic who, did he not really exist, could have been invented by Robert Coover. Like J. Henry Waugh, the hero of Coover's classic, *The Universal Baseball Association*, Bill James eats and breathes diamond dust, keeping a trained eye on box scores, figuring and refiguring statistics, numbering his days with RBIs, ERAs, and HBPs—to name just three of life's more vital signs. But while Coover's Waugh is concerned with a league of his own devising, Esquire's James is forever concerned with the real world, the major leagues.

As I was winding down my senior year of high school, Bill was gaining more of a national footing through his second self-published *1978 Baseball Abstract*, as well as his continued opportunities through magazines. In late April 1979, *Esquire* published its "Baseball '79" issue. Bill's approach in his feature article, "1979 Baseball Forecast," was to predict the season over four glorious pages, by league, division and end-of-season standings, with sound bites about each team. The subtitle of his article captures what readers were treated to: "Remember, you heard it here first: The Tigers have the

Bill James, a twenty-nine-year-old fanatic who gained national exposure. *Author's collection.*

Yanks by the tail; the Reds aren't Rosey; the Bucs get their Phils; the Angels won't fly."[64]

The game of baseball is hard to predict. Bill's prognostications fell short at the end of the year, despite the article's entertainment value. He selected the correct division standing for just eight out of twenty-four teams, while picking correctly only one of four division winners! I had to chuckle at this discovery as I was building a newfound respect for the determination, grit, brilliance, stubborn *persistence* and passion that fueled Bill's efforts over the following decades.

The editor of *Esquire*, in the April 24, 1979, issue, shared great insights on page 6 in Backstage with *Esquire* in his piece titled "Our Crystal Baseball." The image of Bill captures his effervescence perfectly: check him out with his Royals lid on, the *1978 Baseball Abstract* rolled up as if he is waiting for a fastball. His eyes are on fire, framed by oversized glasses, radiating great energy.

> *Like J. Henry Waugh, the hero of Robert Coover's classic,* The Universal Baseball Association, *Bill James eats and breathes diamond dust....* The 1979 Baseball Abstract *has just left Bill James' pocket calculator and typewriter and is about to go to press. Copies should be available by the end of April. They can be ordered directly from Bill James at PO Box 2150, Lawrence, Kansas 66044. The cost is $5.*[65]

I must confess to you that I just put a letter with a check, in the mail, destined for PO Box 2150. While I realize that I am forty-five years late, I cannot wait to get my response!

How did James finally receive tributes like the one from the *Chicago Tribune* that called his *Abstract* the "holy book of baseball?"

His drive to collect, summarize and evaluate baseball data began to capture the attention of not only the first few adopters but also a greater base of fans. Bill continued to write pointed passages illustrating the widespread misunderstanding he felt insiders and fans had about how the game was played. James claimed that the sport was defined not necessarily by its labyrinth of rules but instead by the conditions under which each game was played. He referenced engineering professor Richard J. Puerzer, who shared that the game was "defined by the conditions under which the game is played—specifically, the ballparks but also the players, the ethics, the strategies, the equipment, and the expectations of the public."

*To understand baseball without reference to its statistics is an absurdity…
the only choices are—use the statistics carefully or use them loosely.*[66]

Bill's emerging point of view resulted from early critiques from the baseball world that were directed at him. The words are pointed, dripping with impatience. Case in point, his bluntness is exhibited in the prior quote. A sample of his genius with Sabermetrics was noticed in the *1978 Baseball Abstract*, when Bill shared a belief with the readers that Roger Maris's record of sixty-one homers was breakable. He based this point of view on the idea that George Foster, slugger for the Cincinnati Reds, would have hit sixty-five home runs instead of fifty-two in 1977 if he had played in a normal park. Prescient, right?!

Early adopters of Bill's approach to the game included Sandy Alderson (think Billy Beane, the A's and *Moneyball*), John Henry (stay tuned for Henry to reappear later) and Daniel Okrent (one of the best baseball writers and the creator of Rotisserie Baseball, which exploded on the scene as Fantasy Baseball, eventually becoming a multibillion-dollar industry).

Bill was struggling, putting all his efforts into the *Abstract* work after his normal job hours and not seeing the light of day or his family much, while literally counting his profit in small bills for his 1977–78 work. Dan Okrent gave Bill hope through a letter he wrote, praising him for his work after the second annual publication.

A friendship was engendered. The two were together in 1979, taking in a Twins game, just four days after a sports network called ESPN turned on the studio lights for the first time. Dan was such a believer in what Bill was doing that he pitched a profile on James to *Sports Illustrated*, which did not run the piece until two years later! The Elias Bureau, a staid organization that had a monopoly on official Major League Baseball statistics, had been at battle with Bill over the previous three years, unwilling to share official statistics with him. The bureau was not a fan of the approach Bill was taking through his Sabermetrics discipline—the traditional organization, the protector of baseball statistics as we knew them at the time, kept saying no to Bill.

Coincidentally, the same Elias Bureau was the fact-checker for *Sports Illustrated*'s baseball articles. They had taken offense to Bill's stance with statistics that were included in the Okrent feature article. They forced the hand of *SI*, preventing the feature story from being published.

James continued to plunge into the deep end year after year, grinding through statistical reviews the old-fashioned way to develop new material for *The Baseball Abstract*, which had shifted from self-publishing to Ballantine

Books, a division of Random House. I have a first-edition copy of his 1983 publication that I have packed and moved with my book collection through the years. I love a quote of his from this issue: "This is a book for those who abandon themselves to the game, for those to whom hurried and casual summaries of journalism are a daily affront. It is not for people who already know about baseball, but for those who want to learn."[67]

I picked up my copy in the spring of 1983, months before graduating from the University of New Hampshire with a dual degree in economics and English literature. I was still playing Strat-O-Matic ball with my older brother, Mark, finding the game I'd played for over a decade to be a bridge connecting us in the midst of our adult lives. It was at this moment that I was struck by an epiphany that arrived years too late.

I, too, was a baseball nerd. Every summer morning, I eagerly unfolded the *Boston Globe* sports page to check the baseball box scores and pore over the Red Sox results. Then I would proudly announce the latest updates to my dad through the shower curtain as he prepared for another workday. Today, upon reflection, I know in my heart that I ruined my dad's pleasure in reading the paper cover to cover, since all the baseball news was spit out at him by a ten-year-old determined to get all relevant information to him before the shower head went dry.

I was a Strat-O-Matic dice roller starting in the spring of 1971, when I received a starter game set with the amazing Baltimore Orioles, World Champions led by Brooks Robinson at the hot corner, an early idol of mine. All stat-keeping was done by hand with a worn-out pencil. I used my *Sporting News Batting and Pitching Averages at a Glance*, a three-dollar amalgamation of insights behind each statistical formula and page after page of all potential results, to update team and player statistics.

I was winding down my four-year college journey at UNH with the same two degrees Bill first accomplished.

I was ready to take on the world, a compilation of a baseball nerd, statistical nut and tabletop game solitary dice man indecisive about my next step in life. Why didn't I put two and two together and send Bill James a letter expressing my desire to be his statistical assistant and mentee?

Bill's determination to plow through obstacles was ironclad. He pushed aside naysayers, as underscored by *Boston Globe* sports columnist Dan Shaughnessy, who, in an interview with Rob Neyer, said, "I just don't like statistical-oriented analysis. I think it's overdone. You know what you see. You know the players, you don't know the players, you should stick with that."

Bill's chalkboard formulas. *Courtesy of Megan Day Creations, megandaycreations@gmail.com, Kansas City, MO.*

Sadly, Bill was worn out from years of exhaustion, and his enjoyment in his work was fading fast. His impact was bold, highlighted by the bevy of formulas he developed that baseball fans started embracing versus the traditional batting average, slugging percentage and earned run average as the game-set-match of statistics. Check out the following and tally how many of the new formulas you know and understand!

- RC = runs created = (H+W-CS)*(TB+.7SBs)/(AB+W-CS)
- VORP
- BABIP
- WHIP
- OPS
- WAR
- WS

Bill left a trail of tears, often tears shed by writers and ballplayers whom he lost patience with or who he thought were buffoons or hopeless at the game. Case in point are two examples of his cantankerous prose:

> *What we really need, as I wrote three years ago, is for the amateurs to clear the floor.*[68]
> —*Bill said this while calling out legendary baseball writer Thomas Boswell for his attempt at total average and "big bang theory" metrics.*

> *Doug Flynn does just as much to destroy the Montreal offense as Tim Raines can do to build it.*
> —*Bill shared this in his* 1984 Baseball Abstract.

The exhaustion that Bill experienced resulted from various touchpoints, including his sensitivity to criticism, the battles with his Ballantine editors, excessive book tours, tight deadlines and growing family responsibilities. By late 1985, Bill said, "Some of the fizz had gone out of his writing." And he scrambled to get the *1986 Baseball Abstract* manuscript ready to hand over.

Bill's first days of self-publishing a few hundred copies of his latest opus were joyous in comparison. He was flying under the radar, talking and corresponding with fellow baseball nerds who loved him and working side by side with his wife in his burgeoning cottage industry of Sabermetrics.

Bill's legacy will be with us for years to come. Innovations that he is responsible for include:

- Project Scoresheet, created to counter the Elias Bureau, which became the prototype for numbers-gathering organizations like STATS Inc., Retrosheet and others.
- Strengthening of SABR (Society for American Baseball Research), which is where the term *Sabermetrics* originated from.
- New formulaic approaches to interpreting batting and pitching performance.

Three successful MLB general managers incorporated Bill's work into their general approach with their organizations: John Schuerholz (Atlanta Braves), Sandy Alderson (Oakland A's) and Dayton Moore (Kansas City Royals).

Dayton shared his perspective with me about Bill James and Sabermetrics:

It is always important to have balance in your approach. If you are over-weighted in an area, blind spots tend to be more prevalent. As a GM, it is your responsibility to validate opinions. Utilizing all the data and information allows you to ask the important and necessary questions so you can make a better decision. Every decision we made was put into five basic buckets—there was a scouting judgment, there was character analysis, analytical analysis, financial analysis, and medical analysis. Nobody is right all the time. The organizations that are the most successful are ones that put it all together and utilize all the information. I think Bill James's contributions to the game have certainly been amazing. I am thankful that we have people like him in the game. Some people like to pick one side or the other. I was always very thankful that we had people who looked at the game differently.

Sandy Alderson, who was on the lookout for a "theory of baseball" that could give him an edge, said he found it in the *Baseball Abstract*.

Do you remember my brief mention of John Henry, the billionaire owner of the Red Sox? Before Henry bought his first MLB team, the Florida Marlins, he was entrenched in the world of financial markets, where data replaced beliefs and biases. Henry became a millionaire through his leadership in the sector. He was an early adopter of Bill James, using his findings to absolutely dominate a fantasy baseball league.

Think about the wonderful connectivity in this story. James, through his doggedness and determination, transformed the statistical approach to baseball. Dan Okrent's stubborn resoluteness in the face of doubters who laughed at him when he shared his proposed "rotisserie baseball game," fueled the eventual creation of a billion-dollar business that John Henry, a billionaire himself, thrived in with his determined advocacy of all things Bill James.

Henry and James created a partnership within the Boston Red Sox organization in 2003, when Bill was hired as a consultant to the front office. What happened next? The Red Sox won four World Series titles during the sixteen years that Bill James was part of the organization. Was he responsible for the titles? No. But he definitely influenced the team's approach and actions over the years.

In fact, Bill was credited with standing firm as an advocate for the signing of David Ortiz, the trade for Mark Bellhorn, and the team's stance regarding the importance of on-base percentage. One year later, the Red Sox won their first World Series championship since 1918! Who carried the team on his broad shoulders but "Big Papi"!

In the last few decades, Bill James has rightly been acknowledged for his contributions to the sport. The fusion of his thirst for statistical knowledge and his writing prowess was potent. Bill set the stage for every piece he wrote, starting with a question, studying the issue through statistical analysis and culminating in his uncanny ability to land with a conclusion, blending science and art through his narrative. He attributes his approach to writing to Jim Murray, scribe for *Sports Illustrated*, *Time* and the *Los Angeles Times*, whom he followed closely. Bill's words about Jim Murray are telling when reading any of Bill's two-dozen-plus books: "Murray was a man who wrote with wit and intelligence and a great deal of fire. I came to think it must be wonderful to be able to attack a subject with such weapons as words, images, humor, and bald truth."[69]

In 2006, James was recognized in Time 100 as one of the most influential people across the globe. In March 2017, Bill was honored with the inaugural SABR Analytics Conference Lifetime Achievement Award. As he stepped up to receive the award, which carried more weight for him than the recognition back in 2006, the emcee said, "Perhaps the greatest gift he has is his ability to frame a problem and ask the powerful question, the one no one else oftentimes is asking. He's inspired thousands of others to see an answer that ultimately leads to a much deeper understanding of the game for fans, for baseball operations departments."[70]

The kid from Holton, Kansas, has had quite the journey. The game of baseball is richer because of Bill and his tireless efforts. I thank Bill for entertaining me, exciting me about unusual ways to look at the game and inspiring me to keep rolling the Strat dice!

Let us bring this wonderful story to a close with words that are on page 1 of Bill's *1983 Baseball Abstract*, his seventh annual addition. Peruse this quote, pause quietly to reflect and you will hear Bill drop the mic to the stage before walking off toward a Kansas summer sunset.

> *Hi. My name is Bill James, and I'm an eccentric. If you don't believe I'm an eccentric, just go to the library and look me up. The reason that I am eccentric is that I spend all of my time analyzing baseball games. Well, not all of my time—I have a wife to neglect—but most all of my time. I count all kinds of stuff that lots of people are sort of interested in, but nobody in his right mind would actually bother to count. I devise theories to explain how things in baseball are connected one to another. Once a year I gather all of my notebooks together, translate the work that I have done into English, lash it into some semblance of an organized pattern (I require the help of two editors to accomplish this), and give it to my wife. She types it up or something and sends it off to my publisher. This is called the* Baseball Abstract.[71]

THE UNOFFICIAL KANSAS COLLEGE ALL-STAR ELECTION

DETERMINATION
Staying focused on a plan, even though the path to its end may be different.

I walked into boisterous Fenway Park, next to my two brothers, Mark and Phil, all of us armed with our gloves, ready for almost anything that could happen and shuffling closely to each other as the sounds overwhelmed us. Dad led the way, with us following up the stone steps and taking seats behind the Red Sox bullpen in the bleachers. We did not have a good baseball team, but we loved our Sox, including Sonny Siebert, who was on the mound that Sunday afternoon. I must admit that our priorities eventually shifted from catching home run balls to consuming our popcorn, greasy and warm, stuffed into a cardboard-shaped megaphone with bold print on the outside clearly stating what team we were rooting for.

Once again, the Sox went down despite Sonny's valiant six innings on the mound. All was not lost though. I begged Dad to let us go to the stand where we could grab all-star ballots from a nearby kiosk. During the ride back to Andover, we could debate over our picks prior to making our selections, avoiding hanging chads, oblivious to the stresses and early onset of anger we witnessed as Dad tried to navigate the Volkswagen bus out of Boston. We each pilfered six-cent stamps from the rolltop desk so we could mail off our ballots, our choices going directly to the baseball commissioner at All-Star Election Headquarters. That was a magical day at the ballpark for me.

Why not try to replicate that experience by offering you the opportunity to select your very own Unofficial Kansas College All-Star team? Fill in your ballot! I know you will be surprised at the turn of each page, delving into wonderful sandlot stories across the decades. Witness these Kansas kids as they made the leap from colleges ranging from Wichita State to Washburn University, chasing the elusive dream to play under the big lights. One thing they all had in common was a *determination* to do whatever they could to stay on track to become a big-league ballplayer. The journey, as you have learned in this book, was often not the one the young boys pictured. For some, sadness crept in after years of trying to make it and coming up short, while for others, the journey was one step in their lives, regardless of whether baseball was in their future.

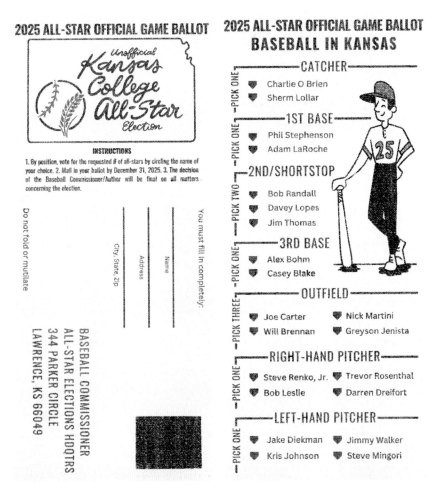

Unofficial Kansas College All-Star ballot. *Courtesy of Megan Day Creations, meganadaycreations@gmail.com, Kansas City, MO.*

Catcher

Charlie O'Brien: Five-year-old Charlie wanted to be Johnny Bench. His catching skills brought him to Wichita State University, where, under the tutelage of Coach Gene Stephenson, he started to refine his game and staff management skills. Over fifteen years of catching in the bigs, Charlie caught for eleven Cy Young Award winners and served as a personal catcher to Greg Maddux in two amazing years with the Braves, where Maddux overwhelmed all batters, delivering a 1.56 and 1.63 ERA in 1994 and 1995. Greg said, "We work well together. I very seldom shake him off. I watch all the catchers on TV closely, and to me, Charlie is easily the best in baseball."[72] Another HOF pitcher, Don Sutton, reflected about O'Brien's skills, sharing that he thought Charlie was born to be a catcher, swallowing pitches with his soft, pillow-like hands game after game. His other claim to fame during his career was brought about by one too many foul tips striking his unprotected head. Charlie looked to the National Hockey League and goalie masks for inspiration for a new mask design. Eventually, MLB approved the use of the design, which protected a catcher's head much better. He debuted his hockey-inspired mask against the Yankees. By the end of the series, catcher Jim Leyritz of the Yankees was hooked, and the trend continued, including an endorsement from Hall of Famer Pudge Rodriguez.

Sherm Lollar: Fate affected Lollar's career, cursed as he was to be in the shadow of Hall of Famer Yogi Berra, who played the same seventeen years that Sherm played. Despite attending a high school that had no baseball team, he was signed in 1943 at eighteen years of age by the minor-league Baltimore Orioles. Two years later, Lollar won the Most Valuable Player Award in the International League, batting .364 while connecting 34 times for home runs. In 1947, Sherm competed with Yogi for the starting role with the Yankees. He finally broke through for good with the White Sox in 1952, becoming their backstop for the next ten years, hitting 124 four baggers, making seven All-Star teams and receiving MVP votes five straight years. Sherm was remembered defensively for his style of catching, with his left knee on the ground in the dust behind home plate, blocking errant pitches. Baserunners were fearful of trying to steal a base through the years, knowing that Lollar nailed just over 46 percent of all base-stealers. Sherm tied a Major League record in 1955, which still stands today, when he had 2 hits in an inning twice in a game versus the Kansas City Athletics.

Lollar batted against four different pitchers in those two innings, singling three times, homering once as the White Sox put up a Bears-like football score, winning 29–6.

FIRST BASE

ADAM LAROCHE: Babe Ruth, Hank Greenberg, Yogi Berra, Johnny Bench, Mike Schmidt and Adam LaRoche have one thing in common that should be celebrated: these six ballplayers homered in each game of a four-game series versus the Chicago Cubs in historic Wrigley Field once in their career. Adam made history and put an asterisk on his series, hitting five homers in total! Adam hails from a baseball family, following in the footsteps of his dad, Dave LaRoche, who pitched in the Major Leagues. LaRoche can look back at several significant accomplishments, including his best year in 1986, when he hit .285, rocketing thirty-two dingers and driving ninety teammates across the plate. Ten years later, Adam announced unexpectedly during White Sox spring training that he was retiring. His reason: family. For years, LaRoche had his oldest son spend time with him on the field and in the clubhouse. Kenny Williams Jr. was general manager for the White Sox. Williams felt that Adam's fourteen-year-old son was a distraction and placed a restriction on his access to the clubhouse. The importance of family overshadowed the $13 million contract. Adam walked away from baseball, shoulder to shoulder with his son.

PHIL STEPHENSON: Phil joined his older brother, Coach Gene Stephenson, at Wichita State in the early years of Shocker baseball's rebirth. Phil's name appears in the NCAA Division 1 record books twenty-five times. Phil put fear in his opponents' hearts, hitting over .400 in three successive seasons, with his best average of .447 boosting his career average to .423. In 1981, he hit in a then NCAA record forty-seven consecutive games, a record that was eventually surpassed by Robin Ventura. He was a two-time All-American and National Player of the Year in 1982. That year, when the Shockers lost in the final game of the NCAA World Series, Phil left it all out on the field, batting .399, while leading the nation with eighty-seven stolen bases. After he was drafted by the Montreal Expos, Stephenson's Major League career was brief and quite different from his days as a collegian. He was named one of the three greatest college baseball players in the twentieth century by Collegiate Baseball and will forever be remembered as a one-man wrecking crew for the Shockers.

SECOND BASE AND SHORTSTOP

BOB RANDALL: In 1976, Twins manager Gene Mauch decided to shift future Hall of Famer Rod Carew to first base, opening second base for Bob Randall. Bob's best year was spotlighted by his .267 batting average and his skills at bunting runners ahead. Randall paid his dues prior to joining the Twins, playing over 700 ballgames in the Dodgers minor leagues, hitting over .300 in four of those years, yet never getting the opportunity to play at Chavez Ravine. Bob revisited the college ranks, winning 475 games as head coach at Iowa State and KU.

DAVEY LOPES: The night before Davey's wedding, he broke up two no-hitters in a 1968 doubleheader while wearing his Daytona Beach Dodgers uniform. Lopes, best known for his stolen base achievements, stole 77 bags while being caught only twelve times in his third season in 1975. Thanks to Manager Tommy Lasorda, who converted Davey from outfield to infield, the legacy left behind by the great Dodger infield of Steve Garvey, Lopes, Bill Russell and Ron Cey stands today. Lopes, the greatest second baseman in Dodgers history, was feared as a lead-off batter, setting a high standard for

Davey Lopes, caught stealing in the 1977 World Series. *Courtesy of Joe Kennedy,* Los Angeles Times.

his running proficiency, stealing 557 bases with an 83 percent success rate. Over his ten-year career with the Dodgers, Davey stole an average of 41 bases a year. Lopes was drafted in 1968, after having a great year at Washburn University in Topeka, where he starred in baseball and played basketball for the Ichabods, graduating with an elementary education degree.

JIM THOMAS: Wichita State would not have become a nationally recognized baseball program without so many great collegiate ballplayers, including Thomas. Jim was destined to play for Stephenson and the Shocker program after graduating from Wichita Southeast High School and leading his undefeated '78 team to a state championship. The team was called the "national champions," as well as one of the greatest collections of high school players of all time. In 1982, Jim led the nation in hits and triples. Thomas further ingrained himself in Shocker baseball history, batting .351 for his career at WSU and eventually joining Gene Stephenson's coaching staff for twenty-one seasons.

THIRD BASE

ALEX BOHM: Alex hit a home run in his first at-bat for Wichita State and went on to become one of the "Bash Brothers" during his Shocker days, sharing the stage with teammate Greyson Jenista. Alex duplicated his first

Alex Bohm, Philadelphia Phillies. *Courtesy of Yong Kim, staff photographer,* Philadelphia Inquirer.

at-bat success, doubling in his first at-bat in the bigs for the Phillies, driving a sharp ground ball over the third base bag. The stadium was full of empty seats during a pandemic year; the iconic Zoom images of his parents and girlfriend cheering him on, smiles and tears mingled, will forever be locked in his memories. The only Nebraska ballplayer to go higher in the draft than Bohm, becoming a Philadelphia Philly in the third round of the 2018 draft, was the Royals' very own Alex "Gordo" Gordon, who went second in the first round of the 2005 draft.

Bohm has been the starter at third for the Phillies since 2022, playing a key role in their success in his first two years. Alex hit a solo home run in the 2022 World Series versus the Astros and Lance McCullers, launching the one thousandth home run in World Series history.

CASEY BLAKE: Casey shares an approach to hitting with one of my all-time favorite Boston Red Sox, Dwight "Dewey" Evans. Both players constantly adjusted their stances, picking up nuances while watching other hitters, trying to find the elusive Shangri-La of hitting. Casey admitted that he was awful about altering his stance as often as he did. Blake said, "It was almost a game-to-game thing."[73] He was named one of the top ten Iowa high school athletes of all time. He went on to star at Wichita State on the field and in the classroom, becoming an Academic All-American twice and a Baseball All-American three times. Drafted by the Blue Jays in 1996, Casey played for Toronto, Cleveland, Baltimore, Minnesota and, finally, the Dodgers, hitting 167 homers over his career. His perspective about his role as his career progressed was to bring more to the team than what transpired on the diamond. Casey's influence became clear over his two years with the Dodgers, where, according to *Wall Street Journal* writer Hannah Karp, he was "one of baseball's least selfish players, quietly hell-bent on smashing conflict, extinguishing outsize egos."[74] Blake and his wife have since created a foundation that has donated over $1 million to his hometown's school district in Indianola, Iowa.

OUTFIELD

JOE CARTER: I had the opportunity to sit with Brent Kemnitz, longtime pitching coach on Gene Stephenson's staff at WSU. He told me that Gene and the staff encouraged their multisport athletes, such as Joe Carter, to play other sports as well as baseball. In the case of Joe Carter, who reported to Shockers baseball practice after the football season concluded, he never looked back at the gridiron once he achieved early success on the diamond and developed into a star. Joe and his teammates immediately helped put the Shockers' fledgling baseball program on the national map. As a freshman, Joe batted .450 while learning the intricacies of playing defense for Wichita State. He was a three-time All American and National Player of the Year in 1981, when he hit .411, setting the then NCAA record, driving in 120 runs while clearing the fences 24 times. Joe became known as the "100-RBI" batter in the bigs, surpassing that number ten times. His shining moment came in 1992, when, with two outs, he hit a World Series–clinching three-run walk-off home run, driving in future Hall of Famers Paul Molitor and Rickey Henderson. The play-by-play man for the Blue Jays, Tom Cheek, shouted exuberantly, "Touch 'em all, Joe! You'll never hit a bigger home run in your life!"[75]

WILL BRENNAN: Will, leading off for the Guardians in Cleveland, hit a sharp grounder that struck and killed a bird. After the game, Brennan posted, "I am truly sorry @peta and bird enthusiasts." He tweeted that "it was an unfortunate sacrifice." The next day, Will hit a home run, later dedicating it to the bird. Brennan is known for more than just this event, as he starred at Kansas State, batting .360 as a freshman All-American. He broke the freshman batting record, hitting in forty-six of the forty-nine games he played in. Will was a two-way player initially, pitching and playing in the outfield. The Blue Valley High School graduate from Overland Park played for the Guardians in 2024, displaying his clutch-hitting ability and versatility, playing all outfield positions. I promise that there are no other All-Star-eligible picks for the "Unofficial Kansas College All-Stars" who have played for not only the Anchorage Glacier Pilots but also the Double-A Akron RubberDucks!

NICK MARTINI: Nick reached base in ninety-three consecutive games while a Wildcat in Manhattan, Kansas. That is not a typo! Martini was drafted in the seventh round, the 230th pick, by the St. Louis Cardinals. He went on to play for the Muckdogs, River Bandits, Chiefs (not of Arrowhead turf!), Cardinals, Redbirds, Sounds, Aviators, Cubs and Bats in his minor-league journey. "Designated for assignment" was a phrase that Nick no doubt despised as he worked his butt off to make it for good at the big-league level. What served as a springboard for Martini was the year he played for the Dinos in the KBO (Korean Professional Baseball League).

As one of the players filling their foreign player quota, he slashed his way to a .296 average, showing power with sixteen home runs and speed with twelve stolen bases. The Cincinnati Reds picked his contract up, and after success at two minor-league stops, Nick made the 2024 roster, hitting two home runs in the season opener. How sweet success is after persevering for so long!

GREYSON JENISTA: This book wouldn't be complete without the presence of a Lawrence kid on the ballot. Greyson starred for three years as a Wichita State Shocker, combining his power with Alex Bohm's to create havoc for opponents. Standing at six feet, four inches tall, Greyson exhibited left-handed power and athleticism that eventually resulted in him playing centerfield. He led the Shockers in hitting in his first two years in Wichita. Greyson put himself on the draft board after being selected as the 2017 MVP of the Cape Cod Summer League. Before he knew it, his new home(s) after being drafted by the Atlanta Braves were with the Danville Braves, Rome Braves, Florida Fire Frogs, Mississippi Braves, Scottsdale Scorpions and Gwinnett Stripers. Despite the grit, energy and enthusiasm he brought to the ball field every day, he was released by the Braves in 2023. The Royals picked up Greyson soon after the Braves let him go, hopeful they could help him develop his hitting to get to the next level. Jenista gave it his

Greyson Jenista, MVP for the Cotuit Kettleers in the Cape Cod League. *Courtesy of* Wichita Eagle *photographer Rick Heath.*

best. Mike Roberts, the manager of the Cotuit Kettleers, in the Cape Cod League, shared that Greyson "played a very good centerfield in the league. You take a really great athlete like Greyson, and you see what can happen. You believe in an athlete and see what he can do."[76]

RIGHT-HANDED PITCHER

STEVE RENKO JR.: Steve Renko takes the snap as quarterback of the KU Jayhawks and hands it off to Gale Sayers, who gains his 917th yard of the 1963 season, finishing with an average of 6.9 yards per carry. Renko strips off his jersey after two years of sharing the backfield with Gale, throwing just three touchdown passes on a team heavily reliant on the running game. End of story, right? Wrong. Starting at guard for your Kansas Jayhawks, Steve Renko! Allen Fieldhouse came alive as Renko joined the other starters before the game. Renko, six foot, four inches tall, led all guards with just under ten points and six rebounds per game for the 1963–64 Jayhawks who finished 13–12, third in the Big Eight Conference. Renko, a senior,

Steve Renko Jr., KU graduate, won 134 Major League games. *Courtesy of the Kansas City Royals.*

took a breather, put his cleats on and then headed to the pitcher's mound for the Jayhawks, where he led the team with a 0.99 ERA and hit .344. What could he not do? Renko was the last athlete to letter in three sports at KU. Odds are that we will never see an athlete achieve this again. Steve collected 134 wins in his Major League career, winning 15 in both 1971 and 1973. Looking back at his career, Renko can recall being drafted by the Oakland Raiders in 1966, working out for Al Davis. Davis offered him a three-year contract, but Steve opted to play baseball. "All you have to do is watch on Sunday afternoons to see that those guys get hurt. Baseball was it."[77]

TREVOR ROSENTHAL: Trevor, a shortstop at Cowley County Community College in Arkansas, Kansas, turned into Rosenthal, a high-velocity All-Star closer with the St. Louis Cardinals for two great years, saving ninety-three games overall in 2014–15. In his career, 70 percent of his saves occurred during those two years of dominance as a closer. Batters did not like digging in to face Trevor, whose pitches were hard to pick up and came at you at over one hundred miles per hour. His average velocity in 2015 was just under ninety-eight miles an hour, which no doubt influenced his low ERA of 2.10. Trevor, the third-youngest pitcher ever to have back to back forty-save seasons, pitched for four additional teams in his last two years in the bigs, including the Washington Nationals, Detroit Tigers, San Diego Padres and our Royals.

DARREN DREIFORT: Darren was drafted second by the Dodgers in the first round behind high school shortstop and phenom Alex Rodriguez. Imagine if A-Rod had played his career with the Dodgers?! Dreifort won forty-eight games in his big-league career. He made his professional debut in the big leagues, pitching an inning of relief against the Miami Marlins. Taking a step back in time, Dreifort was a mammoth talent at Wichita State. In his best year, 1993, Darren finished at 11–1 with a 2.48 ERA, while also hitting .327 with 22 home runs. Sadly, Dreifort ran into overwhelming physical challenges during his career, enduring twenty surgeries over his twelve years of professional baseball.

LEFT-HANDED PITCHER

KRIS JOHNSON: Kris threw five no-hitters in high school. He opted to play in Japan after struggling for two years in the bigs with the Twins and Pirates. In Johnson's inaugural year with the Hiroshima Carp, he finished with a 1.85 ERA, the lowest ever by a foreign player. Kris is the only ballplayer with Kansas roots (and first foreign player) who has won the Eiji Sawamura Award, which is given to the top pitcher in Nippon Professional Baseball. He took the mound in his second year in Japan, compiling a 15–7 record with a stellar ERA of 2.15. Playing in the highest professional league in Japan gave Kris financial security, as he earned more there than he could in the United States. What made this journey wonderful for Johnson were his Japanese family roots, his heritage going back to his paternal grandfather, who had been born in Tokyo.

JAKE DIEKMAN: Mom knew best when it came to Jake and his approach to pitching in the Major Leagues. Months before Jake was drafted by the Phillies, his mom, Billie, died. As we all should consider doing when we lose someone close, Diekman went to counseling as he grieved for his number one cheerleader. To this day, he meditates and thinks about her as the "Star Spangled Banner" is played before his games. In 2024, Jake pitched for his ninth team, the New York Mets, in his twelve-year career. His journey in the game took flight after his sophomore year at Cloud County Community College, when his speed was noticed at a junior college baseball showcase. Jake has won twenty-eight games, primarily pitching in relief as a left-handed specialist.

STEVE MINGORI: "I never thought I would play in the Majors, let alone my hometown." Steve started matriculating at the University of Missouri–Kansas City, finishing his college career pitching for the Pittsburg State Gorillas. In his second season pitching for the Peninsula Grays, a Reds Single A team, Steve witnessed Satchel Paige's final pro start. In an interview with the *Newport Daily News*, he said that he "was in awe of Satchel Paige," going on to say that "he could hit a dime on home plate." The sidearm slinger fell in love with the greatest game played on dirt, pitching for the Royals between 1973 and 1979. Steve's screwball was tough to hit, shaping his 3.03 career ERA.

HOW DID YOU LAND with your outfielders? Who did you select to join Joe Carter? These were the dilemmas that I debated after returning to our home on 62 Elm Street in Andover, Massachusetts, after our 1971 Fenway family outing. Of course, my world view of Major League Baseball was sculpted and refined in those early days through turning the pages of the *Boston Globe*, chewing through the box scores and relishing anything that then *Globe* writer Peter Gammons presented to his fans. (The structure of this chapter is my way of paying homage to the Sunday columns that Gammons was famous for!)

I realize that I leave myself open to challenges regarding the players I offered up as candidates in the election. That is what makes the game of baseball beautiful!

"I'LL CHERISH THIS
THE REST OF MY LIFE"

Bubba Starling's press conference after his first big-league start.[78]

EXCELLENCE
Doing the best that you possibly can.

*What I do know, he was one of the best athletes
I ever saw on a Major League field.*
—*Mitch Webster, Kansas City Royals scout*

Through her years at Madison Elementary School, first grade teacher Linda Morgovnik had the occasional interaction with a new student, typically a young boy, who expressed to her that he wanted to become a professional athlete. In the fall of 1998, one of her taller first-graders, Derek, made it pretty clear to her that when he grew up, he did not want to be a police officer, a firefighter or a teacher. He was going to grow up to be a professional athlete, and he wanted her to call him Bubba, not Derek.

Morgovnik responded, saying to Derek that when he became a famous athlete, she would call him Bubba. Two decades later, Derek was called up to the Royals. His first-grade teacher was one of a legion of Gardner folks who attended one of his early games at the K. "She called me Bubba for the first time," Derek "Bubba" Starling shared with a smile. "How cool is that?"

Bubba's professional baseball career unfolded over eight years, culminating in his first game donning Royals blue, having finally traveled the 35.7 miles from his hometown to the K. Why is Starling's story worth sharing? His journey as a big-league ballplayer, hometown hero and high school legend will inspire us as well as shed light on the difficult road young ballplayers must travel as they strive to play their first game in a Major League uniform.

Why did Derek become Bubba? It began with the arrival of a ten-pound baby boy, a chunky monkey, with legs that appeared game ready for any sport. An aunt of his blessed him officially as "Bubba" the moment she took in his pudgy little legs—the nickname stuck.

His prowess at any sport became legendary in his hometown. At eight years of age, Bubba claimed the mound as one of his favorite spots, throwing darts toward his catcher. Fear paralyzed the young batters—as well as parents—from the opposing team once they witnessed the fastballs let loose by Bubba. Parents complained to Starling's dad that they were scared their kids could be hurt. The young athletic prodigy was moved up to the next age level, landing in the ten-year-old league.

By high school, the six-footer was dominating whatever sport he decided to play. His high school baseball coach implemented a Bubba rule, putting a wood bat in Starling's hands at practices to reduce the distance of his home run blasts that had begun landing in the elementary school parking lot, too close to unsuspecting students leaving the school grounds.

Bubba's parents were believers in their kids staying active, encouraging them to spend idle time outdoors, whether to play catch, hit jump shots or cast a fishing line in a nearby pond. His dad challenged his son to go out and find a ball, no matter what shape it was, to occupy his time—otherwise, his dad would find "something" for him to do. Bubba clearly knew that playing ball was the best option!

His legend grew early in his high school days, his fastball topping ninety miles per hour, a blur streaking past frozen batters. Despite lacking the finesse of a seasoned pitcher, Bubba was as likely to throw a no-hitter or strike out a dozen batters. Starling excelled on the football field as well, striking fear in linebackers and cornerbacks as he tucked the ball under his arm and took off around the end. I watched game videos and was impressed by Bubba, the starting quarterback for Gardner-Edgerton who had a quick release as well as the speed, strength and size that required the opposing defense to gang tackle him.

College and professional scouts started to hear about this Gardner kid and traveled to watch Bubba dominate games, whether it be with a long home run off his bat, a chase after a long fly ball, a tight spiral touch pass or a sprint around an end to find a hole and run over solo defenders. The kid could run the forty-yard dash in just under 4.4 seconds, had a thirty-four-and-a-half-inch vertical jump and could throw a fastball at close to ninety-five miles per hour. He also had the strength to throw a deep ball eighty yards down field to a wide receiver on a slant route.

Mitch Webster, a scout for the Royals, remembers appreciating the athleticism that Starling demonstrated, regardless of the sport he was playing. Webster told me, "I saw Bubba get ten or twelve dunks in traffic in a game, watched him run for 250 yards as a shotgun quarterback. I saw enough of his pure athleticism; he was an unbelievable defensive center fielder, a great runner and had raw power."

Bubba Starling ranks as one of the best high school athletes the state of Kansas has ever witnessed. Selected as an All-State athlete in three sports, he was rated as high as number six in the graduating quarterback class of 2011 and was also touted as the number one high school baseball recruit.

Starling and his parents were presented with two opportunities as Bubba hung up his high school baseball jersey for the last time. He had finished his senior year and achieved greatness in his two primary sports. He ran for 395 yards in a state semifinal in November 2010. Starling, fighting off cramps, could not hear the Blue Valley fans sarcastically cheering their defense as they tackled him for "just" a 9-yard gain. Bubba averaged 14 yards per carry his senior year. Spring and baseball arrived; Bubba dominated batters, intimidating them with his professional-caliber fastballs.

Dayton Moore, who was the general manager of the Royals from 2006 to 2021, shared his thoughts with me about Bubba: "I first met Bubba when he was a sophomore. Bubba was very engaging. He made a great first impression on me personally." Moore went on to share that the Royals' scouting team tried to keep their interest low-key, not wanting to tip their hand to scouts from teams across the country of the Royals interest in Starling.

Meanwhile, college football coaches were extremely interested in Starling for their nationally preeminent programs. Nebraska wedged their way ahead of the pack, chasing Bubba and his family down and offering him a scholarship to come to the university to play not just football but also baseball. It had to have been overwhelming for this talented young man and his parents to be the beneficiaries of such intense interest. The pressure increased when Scott Boras, agent to some of the best ballplayers in the Major Leagues, stepped in to represent Bubba.

Dayton Moore shared his approach to drafting that he brought from his days with the Atlanta Braves to his general manager position with the Royals. He knew that it was critical that the Royals scout as aggressively in their own backyard as they would in the hotbeds of high school talent from southern California to Florida. Dayton shared, "We don't want to get beat in our own backyard. There is no doubt it has more appeal to us as an organization to land a local player, a local talent. This is his boyhood team. This is where he wants to be."

Bubba, with his parents next to him, agreed to terms with the Royals moments before the signing deadline. At the time, the three-year $7.5 million contract he signed was the second largest in draft history. Boras had worked his negotiating magic, witnessing a signing that was the largest ever for a high school player.

Starling was now set up to pursue his first-grade dream, all for his hometown team. Mitch Webster shared that he could not imagine the journey that Bubba was starting, philosophizing about how hard it could be to deal with the local boy–future star billing. Mitch said, "We haven't talked about all the pressure on a local guy. That made the journey twice as hard."

Moore, now a senior advisor of baseball operations for the Texas Rangers, had this to say about where he thought Bubba's mindset was shortly after the signing. "He's going to take that field in the minor leagues every day with that vision of playing here in Kansas City, making his hometown team proud. You need that motivation because it is very difficult to make it to the Major Leagues." Starling's work ethic and drive to achieve *excellence* was exhibited from his first days in the Royals organization.

Bubba hit the ground running with the Burlington Royals. The nineteen-year-old put together a five-game hitting streak in his first seven games played, batting .321 with two home runs and nine RBI'S, fueled by three straight multi-hit games. As the season stretched on, the battle for consistency started, and the roller coaster ride of pressure and disappointment began. How difficult was the trek for Bubba? Starling progressed for eight years through the Royals minor leagues, suiting up for the Burlington Royals, Lexington Legends, Wilmington Blue Rocks and Northwest Arkansas Naturals and, finally, in 2016, getting the promotion to the Triple A Omaha Storm Chasers. Bubba Starling, athlete extraordinaire, had not seen the Kauffman checkerboard outfield grass yet.

Bubba had so much to be proud of at this point in his career, despite his struggles. He was given the opportunity to represent Team USA. He could look back at great memories of when he played for the under-eighteen squad. Proud to represent his country, he batted .399, drove in twelve RBIs, launched three home runs and crossed the plate twenty times.

The grind that ballplayers go through is brutal. "Whether it was my swing or something mentally, every time I got down in the drain, I couldn't get back out," Starling said in an interview with the press at the K.[79] Bubba felt the pressure from day one with the Burlington Royals, playing a tug of war in his mind, thinking that he had to make it to the big leagues in a year. He went on to reflect, sharing, "I was always confident 'no one's' going to beat me coming out of high school. Obviously, it is a different game here, but I got humbled real quick about the failure part of it. And I guess I wasn't mature enough at times to know how to get out of that and how to get through those things."[80]

In this book alone, stories surface about Mickey Mantle coming close to quitting the game twice, Alex Hugo overcoming the new trials transitioning to baseball, and Walter Johnson struggling with his deteriorating skills. Mitch Webster shared the following thoughts with me: "You are talking about Hall of Fame guys that still aren't satisfied because it is stinkin' hard to hit. The mentality of those guys in the big leagues—they are perfectionists to the max. I thank God that I met Jesus when I was younger and had some inner strength. I was wrapped so tight." The internal pressures that all athletes at this level bring on themselves is stunning.

Dayton built on this theme, stating, "First of all, power and speed as a combination is something that is a little rarer in baseball. It takes more time to develop that. It is all about controlling those skills and getting them to be consistent." Moore went on to tell me that it is so important for a ballplayer to not get too high or get too low: "You cannot be successful if you are a perfectionist. The game is going to reward the players who learn to manage the challenges and failures best. It requires so much focus, concentration and mental discipline. It can really mess with you."

Dayton hesitated, thinking about Bubba and his talent, saying, "He could do uncoachable, unteachable things because of his abilities."

In 2017, in Bubba's first full season at Triple A Omaha, he was struggling. He said, "I was swinging at everything. I was striking out a lot. I was just negative."[81] The discipline needed to continue to be consistent, with all aspects of a player's game harmonious, put disproportionate pressure on ballplayers from spring training games to the World Series. The jump to Triple A had him questioning his ability to make it. He texted his mom, a good athlete in her time, to share with her that he might be ready to give it up. He was greeted with a response full of the love and support moms are graced with. Words of wisdom and encouragement popped up on his phone screen: "You are a fighter. You've always grinded your way through things. God has a plan for you. It's a test right now."[82]

Bubba Starling at bat in 2019. *Courtesy of the Kansas City Royals.*

Jumping ahead to 2019, Bubba, after fighting off debilitating injuries for several years, was in the league's Triple A All-Star Game. His stat line over the first seventy-two games of the season was evocative of his best days on the field, with a .310 average and seven home runs. Remember what Dayton Moore said about the challenges that a ballplayer faces when they have both raw power and speed? Moore knows through his years in Major League Baseball that the uphill battle is more difficult for a player like Bubba than it might be for a slashing speedster. Starling was consistently a smart baserunner, stealing bases through his career with an 80 percent success rate, which is amazing, considering his six-foot-five-inch frame that carried close to 220 pounds!

One of the sweetest moments of Bubba's career came during a phone call he placed to his parents at dinner after the All-Star game. Their son shared, "Looks like I won't be flying to Omaha, and I'll be seeing you guys at home. I finally got the call."[83]

Dayton Moore reflected, sharing, "Bubba, Bobby [Witt Jr.] and Adalberto Mondesi are the three best athletes I have ever scouted and signed." When we pause and think about that statement, two of the three ballplayers are not in the game today. The sheer cliff face that a young ballplayer must climb, meticulously, patiently day after day can be overwhelming. The grind and fear of not achieving one's goal is a daily battle. At the end of the day, however, the amazing achievements realized along the way from sandlot play to the big-league stage signify success.

Bubba reflected on his baseball journey as he spoke to the press after his first game roaming centerfield at the K: "I've been waiting for this my whole life, dreamed about it as a little guy growing up coming to ballgames here

Bubba Starling, 2019 Kansas City Royals, after hitting his first home run. *Courtesy of the Kansas City Royals.*

in Kansas City."[84] Starling made a point of thanking then Royals General Manager Dayton Moore and the entire organization for sticking with him, practicing patience and giving him time to grow as a player and as a man.

Bubba built memories that will be with him forever during his time with the Royals, tucking away the recollections of his first big-league hit and his first home run, which was fittingly caught by a fan sporting Royals gear from head to toe. The two Royals united, with the memento thankfully landing in Starling's hands after the game.

Bubba was a legendary high school athlete, wore our country's USA uniform as a teenager and later as an Olympian in the 2020 Summer Olympics held in Tokyo, worked his ass off through the minors and did see his dream come true with his hometown team. I know that if I had the opportunity to read a story like this as an impressionable Little Leaguer with similar dreams, I would be excited and driven to talk about Bubba until the sun fell below the horizon while playing catch with my dad in the backyard.

My conversations with the two men who were instrumental in bringing Starling to the Royals organization illustrate how proud they are of what Bubba accomplished and, more importantly, how disciplined Starling was. Mitch Webster emphasized, "I thought Bubba did a tremendous job every day he was a Royal, trying to make us look good, because of the time and effort we put into him. I always really appreciated it; he really worked his butt off as a Royal." Dayton opened my eyes to the reality that Bubba faced when he came up to the Royals. He talked about the aspect of good or bad timing when a player breaks into the Major Leagues that can help facilitate and springboard or hinder a career at that level. Bubba broke in during a Royals rebuild, feeling the additional pressure of being in the spotlight, with the inability to blend into a lineup full of depth, veteran leadership and a winning atmosphere.

Moore brought it home to me in our first conversation, sharing a phrase that has lingered in my mind: "Success yesterday doesn't guarantee success today, just as failure yesterday shouldn't mean failure today." Dayton speaks from personal experience from his days playing college baseball, as well as the role he plays with his son, Robert, who was drafted by the Brewers in 2022 and is now playing at the Double AA level. Robert's dad said, "If you were able to really connect and have a discussion at a very deep, honest level with many a baseball player, the game can become a burden and emotionally draining to them because of what they are trying to do night in and night out."

Bubba brought discipline, strength, athleticism, confidence in his abilities and an amazing work ethic to the Royals organization. He starred at the international level playing for our country, exhibited true grit through his minor-league years and finally achieved his goal: to play for his Kansas City Royals. Starling should stand tall, gratified that he made it, despite the grind and arduous trek. Today, he is coaching talented young players, inspiring them, sharing experiences and, in return, again finding joy in the game. His legacy will grow as he helps the next generation of baseball players in our state chase their dreams.

Some people don't know how tough baseball really is.[85]
—*Bubba Starling after his first game as a Royal*

CROSSING HOME PLATE

I watched Alex Hugo cross home plate and come to a stop in front of her USA teammates after hitting a three-run home run in the gold medal game versus Team Japan. This was her second home run of the 2024 World Cup Championship. The team responded with fire to her salute after crossing home plate, saluting their captain in return. She had been humbled by her selection as the captain for the World Cup and told me, "It was an honor."

Throughout the chapters of this book, I have been able to rejoice in the game of baseball while also grounding myself and you, the reader, in the simple truth that although it's a beautiful game, it can be hard and cruel as well, like life itself.

"I hated to lose, but it was a good run," Alex shared via text after the USA National Team came up short in the gold medal game, losing to Team Japan, the best ballclub in the world. Alex and her teammates proudly accepted the silver medal at the conclusion of the championship game. The USA women's program has medaled in eight of its nine tournaments. The silver they captured in Thunder Bay is their first since 2014, heralding the team's best finish in a World Cup in ten years.

After receiving their medals, as Alex and her teammates gathered with friends and family to shed tears and share a few intimate words, they were immersed in a world of emotions, including pride for what they had accomplished. Fire burned in their hearts, inspiration from each other fueling the flame that keeps elite athletes like this band of sisters focused on driving their talents and the women's game in the United States to new heights.

Who knows where Alex will take her baseball journey as she and Taylor settle into a new rhythm at home with two their two sons? What I do know is that she will continue to inspire youngsters who want to be like her, filling them with the courage and determination to dream big.

I headed south on I-35 to Wichita, host city for the ninetieth year of the National Baseball Congress World Series in 2024. There, I spent four days in the sun at Eck Stadium, taking in seven games, studying eleven of the sixteen teams competing for the championship. I watched Katie Woods, the first woman to lead this amazing tournament, cover every inch of the grounds at Eck Stadium. Her passion for the event radiated in every conversation I witnessed, whether it was with the coach of the Hays Larks, a kid who was chasing down foul balls, volunteers like Charlie or NBC baseball royalty, including Satchel Paige's and Bobby Boyd's families. In ten days, thirty-five games were played, including thirty-six straight hours of baseball forging through lightning delays and oppressive heat.

College ballplayers from across the United States made up the rosters of the sixteen teams and gave it their all on the diamond. I watched close plays at home; aggressive running; pitches that hit the low nineties; home runs vacate the park, aided by the one-hundred-degree temperatures; and great athletes show off their skills.

In a tournament won by the Hays Larks for the first time, after competing in their thirty-eighth World Series over a span of seventy years, my only regret is that the stands were not full of baseball fans. This tournament, put on the map back in 1935 with the help of Satchel Paige, is a diamond in the rough. I live for the day when the tournament gets the attention it deserves, key games coming to us via ESPN as we watch the best college players across the country come together to play baseball, America's national pastime, in America's heartland.

Baseball, as we have seen, comes together over nine innings, a season, a career full of agony, ecstasy and everything in between.

On August 5, 2024, I witnessed a day of healing, hope, resilience and community at the unveiling of the new Jackie Robinson statue.

Bob Lutz opened the ceremony by summoning his League 42 ballplayers: "All of our players, come up to the front so you can see. This is about you." Bob continued to emcee the celebration, introducing Wichita politicians; Bob Kendrick of the Negro League Baseball Museum; Tony Reagins, MLB's chief baseball development officer; retired pitching great C.C. Sabathia; and, finally, eight-year-old Marcus Jones to the podium.

What was reinforced in the pavilion honoring Jackie Robinson, which celebrates the nine powerful values that have resonated through this book, was the interconnectedness of those involved in the game of baseball and the importance of our youth, who play in sandlot fields across our state, country and globe.

Brandon Johnson, Wichita's District One city council member, raised the roof, exclaiming, "This is a great day for Wichita! This is about the young people we see in their League 42 uniforms. The statue is back!"

Bob Kendrick reminded everyone in attendance of an important life lesson, stating, "We know that out of darkness comes light. I think we were able to bear witness to that. I hope that this will serve as an inspiration to the young people today."

The "heinous act" that occurred in January 2024 was perpetrated by a man addicted to fentanyl; he was looking to sell the scrap metal that once was Jackie to fuel his addiction. This man revealed his deep sense of embarrassment and shame. His afflictions are not representative of who he is as a human being. The tragic event, the guilty party, all fit into our dysfunctional national discourse, which is bigger than baseball—the scourge of mental health and addiction in desperate need of government funding and prioritization to help make our world a kinder, better place for all.

Baseball, a game played by kids, from farms in Kansas to League 42 action in Wichita, brings us together as a community. That is the beauty of sports in our culture.

Tony Reagins, representing the high offices of MLB, expressed these feelings beautifully as he shared, "Our hope is that the thousands of young people that utilize the Leslie Rudd Learning Center across the street and the many thousands of young people that will play on these ballfields behind us will come to know how baseball, how this community, how this country, even the world, rallied around a tremendous wrong and made it right."

The park was host to people of all ages for this event—families, the kids of League 42, volunteers, NBC national news reporters, MLB members, fans of the game, the older generation, the next generation. It was the silver lining that Bob Lutz called "an incredible, positive, joyful experience."

C.C. Sabathia connected big-league ballplayers like himself to the grassroots nature of League 42, sharing, "Growing up as a kid in Vallejo, California, I would have been playing in League 42."

Jackie Robinson stands tall once again. *Courtesy of Wichita photographer Christopher Clark.*

Bob brought the ceremony to a close, while I wrote the last words of this book in parallel fashion, by saying to the kids in uniform, "This is your moment." Marcus Jones, the eight-year-old League 42 ballplayer, said that Jackie Robinson, the man who broke the MLB color barrier, was "one of the greatest players of all time. And he put a spark in us."

The canvas was pulled off the shoulders of Jackie, standing proud and tall in bronze, the sky awash with strokes of sunset paint, bat in his hand, the barrel resting on his shoulder. His eyes, laser focused under his Brooklyn cap were looking not only at McAdams Park, where the kids from League 42 play ball and dream big, but also farther out toward the horizon, stretching his shadows, his values, his love for the game across the Sunflower State. The spirit of no. 42, strong and courageous, resonates through sandlot fields, minor-league venues and Major League ball parks where people of all ages play baseball, our American game.

GIVING BACK

How to Support League 42™

In-kind donations of goods and services, as well as donations of time and equipment, are vital to League 42's success.

League 42 is a nonprofit organization, so we rely on our volunteers and donors to make each baseball season happen. We are consistently in need of coaches and team ambassadors to oversee our teams. And we value the volunteer efforts of individuals who assist us with uniform distribution, special events and other activities. If you would like to volunteer for League 42, contact league42wichita@gmail.com or call 316-655-1028.

Whether you have an hour or a year, $5 or $50,000, your passion for baseball can make a difference in a child's life and the Wichita community. We would love to share more details with you. If your church, school, business or civic organization would like a League 42™ representative to make a presentation to your group, we would be thrilled to make that happen. For more information about getting involved in League 42™, please call us at 316-655-1028 or email league42wichita@gmail.com.

Above: League 42 logo. *Courtesy of League 42, Wichita, KS.*

We accept donations of equipment year-round. Our greatest need is youth baseball gloves, new or gently used, as well as other baseball equipment, such as bats, helmets, catcher's gear, etc. Any donations can be dropped off at McAdams Park Recreation Center or by calling 316-655-1028, and we will make arrangements to come to pick them up at your location.

NOTES

INTRODUCTION

1. League 42 Foundation, https://league42.org.
2. Robinson, *Jackie's Nine*, 5.

CHAPTER 1

3. League 42 Foundation.
4. Rudd Foundation, https://ruddfoundation.org; Rudd Foundation, "Leslie Rudd Education Center," https://ruddfoundation.org/programs#league-42.
5. Rudd Foundation, "Rudd Scholarships at Wichita State University," https://ruddfoundation.org/for-students.

CHAPTER 2

6. Thomas, *Walter Johnson*, 41.
7. Thomas, *Walter Johnson*, 42.
8. Thomas, *Walter Johnson*, 202.
9. Clipping, source unknown, n.d., scrapbook IX (1924); Thomas, *Walter Johnson*, 222.

10. Thomas, *Walter Johnson*, 241.
11. Donald Honig, *The October Heroes* (University of Nebraska Press, 1996), 249.
12. *Washington Post*, April 15, 1910.
13. *Washington Post*, April 15, 1910.
14. *Washington Times-Herald*, April 13, 1913.
15. *Washington Times-Herald*, April 16, 1924.

CHAPTER 3

16. Wikipedia, "Wichita Monrovians," https://en.wikipedia.org/wiki/Wichita_Monrovians.
17. Phyllis Wheatley's Children's Home, "About Us," https://wch.org/about-us.
18. *Wichita Beacon*, July 20, 2022.
19. Wikipedia, "Ackerman Island," https://en.wikipedia.org/wiki/Ackerman_Island.
20. Baseball History Comes Alive, "Ron Bolton," https://www.baseballhistorycomesalive.com.
21. Heiman, *When the Cheering Stops*, 146.
22. Heiman, *When the Cheering Stops*, 147.

CHAPTER 4

23. Rives, *Baseball in Wichita*, 65.
24. Tom Shine, "Why Satchel Paige Might Be the Most Significant Figure in Wichita's Baseball History," KMUW, April 1, 2023.
25. Rives, *Baseball in Wichita*, 66.
26. Rives, *Baseball in Wichita*, 66.
27. Travis M. Larsen, "Ahead of the Curve: A History of the National Baseball Congress Tournament in Wichita, Kansas, 1935–2005" (master's thesis, Fort Hays State University, 2006).
28. Larsen, "Ahead of the Curve."
29. Larsen, "Ahead of the Curve."

CHAPTER 5

30. John G. Hall, *Majoring in the Minors* (Oklahoma Bylines, 2000), 166.
31. Hall, *Majoring in the Minors*, 158.
32. Hall, *Majoring in the Minors*, 149.
33. Hall, *Majoring in the Minors*, 151.
34. *Commerce News-Post*, September 15, 1949.
35. Leavy, *Last Boy*, 17.

CHAPTER 6

36. *Hutchinson News*, May 1, 1943.
37. Gordon Olson, All-American Girls Professional Baseball League Collection: Interview with Joyce Barnes McCoy, Grand Valley State University, September 27, 2009.
38. "Glamor Girls for Softball," *Hutchinson News*, May 1, 1943.
39. "Glamor Girls for Softball," *Hutchinson News*.
40. "Glamor Girls for Softball," *Hutchinson News*.
41. Olson, Interview with Joyce Barnes McCoy.
42. Madden, *Women of the All-American Girls Professional Baseball League*, 251.
43. Wikipedia, "National Pro FastPitch," https://en.wikipedia.org/wiki/National_Pro_Fastpitch.
44. USA Women's National Baseball Team, https://www.usabaseball.com/team/womens.
45. Wikipedia, "MLB Home Run Derby X," https://en.wikipedia.org/wiki/MLB_Home_Run_Derby_X.

CHAPTER 7

46. Team Color Codes, "Wichita State Shockers Color Codes," https://teamcolorcodes.com/wichita-state-shockers-color-codes/.
47. Wikipedia, "Bacone College," https://en.wikipedia.org/wiki/Bacone_College.
48. Tom Shine, "Shocks Club Sun Devils in Double-Header Sweep," *Wichita Beacon*, May 10, 1982.
49. Bill MacKay, "NEW WSU Baseball Coach Pledges Winning Teams," *Wichita Eagle*, February 12, 1977.

50. Kansas Historical Society, "Karl T. Wiedemann Foundation," https://www.kshs.org/p/k-t-wiedemann-foundation/19129.

CHAPTER 8

51. Matthew 16:26 (King James Version).
52. *Chicago Tribune*, "8-8-88: The First Night Game at Wrigley," April 1, 2014, https://www.bing.com/videos/riverview/relatedvideo?q=8-8-88+cubs+game&mid=420BDF443F28D93BF348420BDF443F28D93B F348&FORM=VIRE.
53. Blair Kerkhoff, "Can You Imagine a 16-Year-Old Playing in the Majors? This Rockhurst Grad Did, for the KC Athletics," *Kansas City Star*, June 8, 2018.
54. Kerkhoff, "Imagine a 16-Year-Old Playing in the Majors?"
55. Edwin Tracey, "At a Dress Rehearsal of the Champion Giants," *New York Times*, April 16, 1905.
56. David Waldstein, "From Kansas to Giants, a Pioneer's Trail of Wins and Wit," *New York Times*, October 22, 2014.
57. Tracey, "Dress Rehearsal."
58. Ritter, *Glory of Their Times*, 101.
59. Honus Wagner, "Rookies Ran the Gauntlet," *Telegraph-Herald*, March 6, 1936.
60. Sam Molen, "Signing Off," *Baseball Digest*, May 1953.
61. Kansas State School for the Deaf, https://www.ksdeaf.org.

CHAPTER 9

62. Bill James, "Winning Margins: A New Way to Rate Excellence," *Baseball Digest*, November 1975.
63. Society for American Baseball Research, "A Guide to Sabermetric Research," https://sabr.org/sabermetrics.
64. Bill James, "1979 Baseball Forecast," *Esquire*, April 24, 1979.
65. James, "1979 Baseball Forecast."
66. Gray, *Mind of Bill James*, 37.
67. James, *Baseball Abstract*, 2.
68. Gray, *Mind of Bill James*, 52.
69. Gray, *Mind of Bill James*, 117.
70. Society for American Baseball Research, "Bill James Honored with Inaugural SABR Analytics Conference Lifetime Achievement Award,"

March 10, 2017, https://sabr.org/latest/bill-james-honored-with-inaugural-sabr-analytics-conference-lifetime-achievement-award/.
71. James, *Baseball Abstract*, 1.

CHAPTER 10

72. "Sizzling Maddux Rolls On," *Columbia* (SC) *State*, September 1, 1995.
73. Casey Blake interview with Don Doxsie, October 31, 2014.
74. Hannah Karp, "Casey Blake: The Dodger Diplomat," *Wall Street Journal*, October 20, 2009.
75. DiManno, *Glory Jays*, 286.
76. Paul Suellentrop, "Shocker's Jenista Shows MVP Grit in Cape Cod League," *Wichita Eagle*, August 6, 2017.
77. Kansas University Athletics, "Throwback Thursday: Steve Renko Jr.," May 24, 2012.

CHAPTER 11

78. James Wooldridge, "Bubba Starling on Royals Debut," Kansas City Star, July 12, 2019.
79. Lynn Worthy, "Bubba Starling Is Bashing Early for Royals in Spring Training," *Kansas City Star*, February 26, 2019.
80. Vahe Gregorian, "What Bubba Starling Learned on the Long and Winding Road to Home," *Kansas City Star*, February 2, 2020.
81. Gregorian, "What Bubba Starling Learned."
82. Gregorian, "What Bubba Starling Learned."
83. Lynn Worthy, "Royals' Bubba Starling Waited His Whole Life for This Day," *Kansas City Star*, July 12, 2019.
84. Worthy, "Starling Waited."
85. "Bubba Starling Makes Major League Debut with Royals," *USA Today*, July 12, 2019.

SELECTED BIBLIOGRAPHY

INTERVIEWS

Hugo, Alex. June 2024.
James, Deborah. June 2024.
Kemnitz, Brent. May 2024.
Kimbrell, Anne. June 2024.
Luck, Bob. June 2024.
Moore, Dayton. April 2024.
Nelson, Curt. May 2024.
Stephenson, Gene. July 2024.
Webster, Mitch. June 2024.
Woods, Katie. May 2024.

BOOKS

Alexander, Charles C. *Ty Cobb*. Oxford University Press, 1984.
Bailey, John W. *Kenosha Comets 1943–1951*. Badger Press, 1997.
Batting and Pitching Averages at a Glance. The Sporting News, 1967.
Broeg, Bob. *Memories of a Hall of Fame Sportswriter*. Sagamore Publishing, 1985.
Brown, John E. *Wichita State Baseball Comes Back: Gene Stephenson and the Making of a Shocker Championship Tradition*. The History Press, 2014.
Deford, Frank. *The Old Ball Game*. Grove Press, 2005.

DiManno, Rosie. *Glory Jays: Canada's World Series Champions*. Sagamore Publishing, 1993.

Dunkel, Tom. *Color Blind: The Forgotten Team That Broke Baseball's Color Line*. Atlantic Monthly Press, 2013.

Fruth, Jean. *Grassroots Baseball: Where Legends Begin*. Sports Publishing, 2019.

Gray, Scott. *The Mind of Bill James: How a Complete Outsider Changed Baseball*. Doubleday, 2006.

Hall, John G. *Mickey Mantle: Before the Glory*. Leathers Publishing, 2005.

Heiman, Lee. *When the Cheering Stops*. MacMillan Publishing Company, 1990.

James, Bill. *The Bill James Baseball Abstract—1983*. Ballantine Books, 1983.

Leavy, Jan. *The Last Boy: Mickey Mantle and the End of America's Childhood*. Harper Perennial, 2011.

Lewis, Michael. *Moneyball: The Art of Winning an Unfair Game*. W.W. Norton, 2004.

Madden, W.C. *The Women of the All-American Girls Professional Baseball League: A Biographical Dictionary*. McFarland, 2005.

Mantle, Mickey, and Robert Creamer. *The Quality of Courage: Heroes in and out of Baseball*. Bison Books, 1999.

Nowlin, Bill. *SABR 50 at 50*. University of Nebraska Press, 2020.

Povich, Shirley. *The Washington Senators*. Kent State University Press, 2010.

Riley, James A. *The Biographical Encyclopedia of the Negro Baseball Leagues*. Carroll & Graf, 2002.

Ritter, Lawrence S. *The Glory of Their Times*. William Morrow, 1992.

Rives, Bob. *Baseball in Wichita*. Arcadia Publishing, 2004.

Robinson, Sharon. *Jackie's Nine: Jackie Robinson's Values to Live By*. Scholastic Press, 2001.

Schulz, Charles M. *Sandlot Peanuts*. Holt Rinehart Winston of Canada, 1977.

Sumner, Jan. *Independence, Mantle, and Miss Able*. JaDan Publishing, 2015.

Thomas, Henry W. *Walter Johnson: Baseball's Big Train*. University of Nebraska Press, 1998.

Treat, Roger L. *Walter Johnson: King of the Pitchers*. Julian Messner, 1948.

NEWSPAPERS

Andover Townsman
Columbia State
Commerce News-Post
Hutchinson News

Kansas City Star
New York Times
USA Today
Wall Street Journal
Washington Post
Washington Times-Herald
Wichita Beacon
Wichita Eagle

MAGAZINES

Baseball Digest
Esquire
The Sporting News

ARCHIVAL SOURCES

Grand Valley State University–Digital Collections, University Libraries. Allendale, MI.
Independence Historical Museum. Independence, KS.
The Kansas City Royals Hall of Fame. Kansas City, MO.
Kansas Sports Hall of Fame. Wichita, KS.
Negro Leagues Baseball Museum. Kansas City, MO.
Wichita Baseball Museum. Wichita, KS.

ABOUT THE AUTHOR

Michael's love for baseball began in 1967, during a hot August night at his family's lakeside cabin. He listened to Ned Martin and Ken Coleman narrate a Red Sox win at Fenway Park. Yaz, third in the league in batting at .321 and second in homers with twenty-eight, nailed Kansas City A's Mike Hershberger, who tried to score from second on a single. The Sox were just two games behind Chicago in the standings after the 5–3 win. Was the impossible just a dream?

Michael's childhood in Andover, Massachusetts, was loaded with baseball memories, the pomp and circumstance of opening day in the Little League season, the drama linked to a roll of the dice while playing Strat-O-Matic baseball, the daily consumption of the *Boston Globe* baseball news and the endless summer days of playing wiffle ball with his childhood buddy Charlie.

Michael's days of playing ball are in the past, but the deep connection to the game is ever-present, whether he is at a ball game at Eck Stadium or turning pages of *Shoeless Joe*, a 1982 classic by W.P. Kinsella. Michael's better half in life, Ivy, is in pursuit of her master's mental health PA degree while helping those in need as a charge nurse. Michael and Ivy spend idle time enjoying their grown daughters, Katie and Meg, as well as their son-in-law, Chris, and their three grandchildren, all angels, Jude, Luna and Jonah. Of course, one cannot forget that Maci, their goldendoodle, is the queen of their castle in Lawrence, Kansas.

Baseball in Kansas is Michael's second book to be published. He pursued his love of Kansas craft breweries and their communities and stories in his first book, *Celebrating Kansas Breweries: People, Places & Stories*, published in 2022.

Michael's love for the great game of baseball, the thrill of unearthing stories that need to see the sunshine and the joy of writing have come together in his first baseball book. Stay tuned for his next journey around the bases!